# COUNTRY GARDENING

# COUNTRY *Gardening*

## DESIGN IDEAS AND A PRACTICAL GUIDE

BY THEODORE JAMES, JR.

PHOTOGRAPHS BY HARRY HARALAMBOU

HARRY N. ABRAMS, INC., PUBLISHERS

FOR OUR DEAR FRIEND
*Roz Cole*

Page 1: The perfect country garden: an informal flower bed surrounded by a split-rail fence, with a view of a nearby hay pasture and distant mist-covered mountains.
Page 2-3: A smart young fellow has found the perfect spot for reading. He's not distracted by the sun-dappled meadow on the other side of a simple perennial bed.
Page 5, top to bottom: A monarch butterfly finds a bed of zinnias; a stone angel meditates under a spray of white roses; a fine pot dresses up a shady bed of ferns; angel's trumpet on the patio is beautiful by candlelight.

EDITOR: ERIC HIMMEL
DESIGNER: DARILYN LOWE CARNES

Library of Congress Cataloging-in-Publication Data
James, Theodore.
    Country gardening : design ideas and a practical guide / by Theodore James, Jr.;
  photographs by Harry Haralambou
      p.   cm.
    Includes bibliographical references (p. ).
    ISBN 0–8109–4120–1
    1. Landscape gardening–United States.  2. Gardens–United States–Design.
  I. Haralambou, Harry. II. Title.
    SB473.J24 2000
    712'.6'0973–dc21                          99–56543

Printed and bound in China

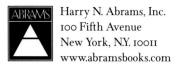

Harry N. Abrams, Inc.
100 Fifth Avenue
New York, N.Y. 10011
www.abramsbooks.com

# Contents

A COUNTRY GENTLEMAN    7

A SENSE OF PLACE    13

GARDEN ARCHITECTURE    29

COUNTRY SEATS    53

WHIMSY IN THE GARDEN    65

WATER GARDENS AND POOLS    79

VEGETABLE GARDENS    95

COUNTRY GARDENING: A BRIEF PRACTICAL GUIDE    103

First Things First: Accessing the Site 103 • Selecting Trees and Shrubs 104 •

Perennials 106 • Planting and Maintaining Hardy Plants 109 • Growing Annuals 111 •

Bulbs 114 • Growing Vegetables 116 • Do-It-Yourself Water Gardens 118 •

Wildlife in the Garden 120 • A Word About Pests and Lyme Disease 124

PLANT LISTS 129

Annuals 129 • Berries 134 • Bulbs 136 • Ferns 142 • Grasses 143 • Ground Covers 145 •

Herbs 147 • Perennials 150 • Roses 159 • Shrubs 161 • Trees 169 • Vines 174 • Water Plants 176

SOURCES 179

ACKNOWLEDGMENTS 180

INDEX OF PLANT NAMES 181

Among the many joys of visiting and driving through the countryside are the views from the roadside. Here two Shetland ponies graze next to a lovely watering hole at a picturesque farm in New England.

# A Country Gentleman

IN ENGLAND THEY SAY THAT YOUNG MEN LEAVE THE COUNTRY AND GO TO THE BIG CITY so that they can make their fortunes only to move back to the country, which they never should have left in the first place. Despite my not having made my fortune, about twenty years ago or so I decided to buy a house in the country. My Manhattan apartment was a green paradise, with houseplants by the hundreds everywhere. It had begun to be ridiculous, and I realized that more than anything I wanted to have a house of my own and a plot of ground on which I could grow more than just houseplants.

One day I ventured out to the North Fork of Long Island, somewhere in the mid-Atlantic, according to my late father, found my dream house, and bought it. It is a modest eighteenth-century house, which recently, thanks to my restoration efforts, has been designated a landmark. This gives me particular satisfaction, because when I bought the place everyone thought I had gone stark raving mad. "It needs so much work," they said. "The support beams are going to collapse," they said. "It needs a new roof," they said. Others patronized me. "It does have charm, doesn't it?" This included my dear late mother, who burst into tears the first time she and my dad came out to take a look at it.

The house in Peconic, New York, was surrounded by an acre of ground. Directly, I passionately embraced my gardening interest and set out to landscape my property. I had grown up in New Jersey in an area that was semi-rural but now is suburban, so I had some experience growing things. Although I was blessed with the best soil this side of Kansas—four feet of topsoil—with the exception of one monumental hundred-year-old yew and a magnificent hundred-and-fifty-year-old copper beech there was nothing else on the property but countless "junk" trees and overgrown bushes. I'm not complaining. The two fine old specimens are indeed rare, and had the previous owner known of their value, he could probably have asked for and received twice the price I paid for the property. I cherish these trees and will be grateful until the day I die to the fine old gentleman who planted them more than a century ago. (I took the time to find out who he was from elderly neighbors, who knew his children and grandchildren.)

Well, the years have flown by, and I expect, by stretching it just a mite, I am a "country gentleman," which out here means that at least once a year I do wear shoes and a necktie. This also means that, like my neighbors, everybody uses my back door. The front door hasn't been opened for more than twelve years. The car keys are practically rusted into the ignition. In the country we never remove them. The key to the house is tucked away somewhere. We don't lock our houses out here. I loathe perfect suburbanlike green lawns that stretch right out to the street. Like most of my friends and farmer neighbors, I am a gardener, and I have a sacred respect for the good earth and what it provides. Therefore, I usually have dirt under my fingernails, a true status symbol for serious gardeners. And yes, I have had Lyme disease. Anyone who hasn't can't possibly be taken seriously as a gardener. I have grown to love the noisy chatter of the birds in the morning. This is partially because I now go to bed around 10 P.M. and get up around 5 A.M., about the same time the birds start chirping.

I have learned to accept and understand the universal life cycle: birth, life, health, sickness, and death. As a gardener I am surrounded by this every day. Plants emerge from seeds and eventually die of old age, just as we do. Plants get sick and then they recover, just as we do. I have a humble perspective about my place on this earth. I now know that I'm not such a big shot after all but just another one of God's creatures. I have learned that the food I grow myself tastes better than what is available in the stores. Perhaps this is because of the holistic aspect of planting seeds, watching them germinate, nurturing the plants, and finally enjoying the harvest. I have found peace of mind, tranquillity, gratification. All of these can be yours as well, if you immerse yourself in nature.

The garden here is a joint effort. My colleague and friend, photographer Harry Haralambou, who did all of the photographs for this book and others that we have written, is passionately involved in the garden. It is truly a collaborative effort, with both of us complementing each other's particular areas of expertise, all in quest of a dazzling garden.

In closing, remember that a real gardener is somewhat different from a homeowner who has a garden that has been designed, installed, and maintained by professionals. Professionally installed gardens are indeed lovely, and often homeowners simply do not have the time to plant their own gardens, hence they hire others to do it. Even if you turn your garden over to a designer to begin with, however, you should treat it as an on-going creative endeavor and become a real gardener.

Since you have a house in the country, real gardening should be your pursuit. And, hopefully, this book will help you achieve your goals. Always remember that a real gardener is never finished. There is always something left to do or something left to change. My dear friend, the late Frances George, was a real gardener who knew that a garden is never finished. Toward the end of her life, she and her daughter were discussing where she wanted her ashes to be strewn. Her daughter suggested our garden because her mother loved it so. Frances said, "Yes, it's very beautiful and I do love it, but they're always digging things up over there."

Seen through an old twelve-paned window is a view of Nancy Gilbert and Richard Wines's meadow garden and barn in Jamesport, New York. The two collect old buildings, and this one belonged to Richard's great-great-great-great-grandfather back in the late eighteenth century.

Burlap potato sacks drying in the sun are a familiar sight on the North Fork of Long Island. Tidy farmers wash them out and recycle them for another crop of potatoes.

Landscape designer Wes Rouse of Southbury, Connecticut, has installed a cobblestone pathway and large swinging gates at the entrance to his elaborate country garden. On the right is his white garden, which is accented by only "true blue" flowering plants. Often flowering plants that are described as having blue blossoms are much more magenta or purple than blue, resulting in what I call "hodgepodge magenta." However, there is a reasonable variety of "true blue" plants available to country gardeners.

# A Sense of Place

UNKNOWINGLY, MANY COUNTRY GARDENERS EMPLOY AN ANCIENT JAPANESE GARDEN principle called "borrowed landscape." This means taking advantage of sweeping views, such as distant stands of trees, and incorporating them into one's own landscape by framing and screening them with trees or shrubs on your own property. The experienced gardener always uses existing old apple orchards, cow pastures, preferably with grazing guernseys, distant mountains, and gentle streams or rivers as part of his or her own personal landscape. Rather than flattening out slopes, use them and incorporate them in a landscape. The same goes for existing structures, distant buildings, granite-strewn fields. The lesson here is to enhance and become part of a landscape rather than imposing on that landscape.

*Opposite:* Designer Peter Dunlop's country house is perched on an aerie in Patterson, New York, overlooking the foothills of the Berkshires. He planted this shady nook with impatiens, Japanese painted fern, various hosta, and shade-loving moss. Nearby is a small waterfall and pond, where armies of frogs splash about and croak.

*Right:* In their extraordinary garden in St. Michaels on Maryland's Eastern Shore, Randy and Dot Rose underplanted an ancient red maple with cerise impatiens, pachysandra, boxwood, and azalea. In the distance is a Japanese maple, always useful for adding an elegant touch to a landscape.

Perhaps nothing says "country" more than an old apple orchard. Here in East Dorset, Vermont, designer Paul Marchese has installed a border of unpretentious, old-fashioned perennials to set off the orchard at the residence of Eric Nisenson and Marla Daniels. In the foreground are Shasta daisies, coreopsis 'Moonbeam,' monarda 'Croftway,' among others. An old orchard offers glorious springtime apple blossoms and if you're lucky, bluebirds will nest because old apple trees are their favorite nesting site. If you care for your orchard by maintaining a regular spray program during the spring and summer, you will have bushels of delicious fresh, crispy apples. That should make anyone happy. Except, of course, people who don't like apples.

Informality is the key word when it comes to country living. And this garden, designed by Sanford Kempner, reflects the informal ambience. The scene is set by two grasses: maiden grass and zebra grass. The trees are wild choke cherries (*Prunus virginiana*), a native plant usually removed; however, it is appropriate in a country garden. Assorted canna lilies, salvia 'Vicki Blue,' salvia 'Indigo Spires,' salvia 'Purple Majesty,' *Salvia leucantha*, rudbeckia 'Irish Eyes,' and sedum 'Autumn Joy' complete the picture.

One of the most beautiful trees available to gardeners is the white birch. A small clump will eventually top off at around thirty-five feet. Here at the Nisenson-Daniels garden, designer Paul Marchese has complemented the tree with an elegant white fence. Old-fashioned perennials, such as daylilies, white Shasta daisies, and hostas, are at home here.

*Left:* This spectacular perennial garden in a meadow at Mr. and Mrs. Robert Ferguson's house in Dorset, Vermont, provides a wonderful display of color from spring through fall. Lythrum 'Morden's Pink,' various hostas, and deep burgundy daylilies are in bloom. Designer Paul Marchese created the garden.

*Opposite:* Charles Lauren of Dorset, Vermont, is a dedicated gardener who at the age of ninety-two still spends a great deal of time maintaining his garden. A small stream meanders through the property. Here yellow *Corydalis lutea* and pink daylilies frame an outcropping of rocks, which are covered with hens and chickens.

*Left:* Who says you can't grow anything in the shade? This is landscape designer Wes Rouse's stunning shade garden in Southbury, Connecticut. Rouse combines tropical plants in containers with all manner of hardy perennial shade-loving plants and annuals. The terra-cotta pots contain a pot fuchsia called 'Thalia,' which Rouse winters over indoors, hardy hosta, annual coleus, and other plants with interesting foliage.

*Above:* Here's an enchanting woodland path, designed by Conni Cross. In the spring, azalea 'Coral Bells' dominates the scene, along with a pink rhododendron. Sweet woodruff flanks the path, adding its intoxicating scent to the garden. This, by the way, is the herb that the Germans use to flavor may wine. Cross has placed two lovely blue vases in view to add visual interest. The small tree is a green Japanese maple *(Acer japonica* var. *acontifolium).*

19

Arthur Ross's garden in Garrison, New York, is a seemingly endless maze of meandering paths. Included in this tree-shaded area are ferns, lilies of the valley, azaleas, various grasses, and the plant that was so popular in American suburbia during the 1950s, pachysandra, used as a ground cover. Many designers and sophisticated gardeners look down their noses at pachysandra. I don't. It is a useful, easy-to-maintain, and very responsible plant. Whenever my late mother would visit with friends back in the 1940s and 1950s, she would always bring a pailful of pachysandra with her for them to plant. It got to the point where she was nicknamed "Our Lady of the Pachysandra."

Here designer Wes Rouse has moved the "foundation planting" of dwarf conifers away from the house, creating a sense of enclosure that is not claustrophobic. Pink cleome and sedum 'Autumn Joy' add just the right dash of color at the Behnke-Dougherty property in Southbury, Connecticut.

Appropriately enough, Randy and Dot Rose of St. Michaels, Maryland, planted an English cottage garden around a small cottage. Daylilies, hostas, and lythrum 'Morden's Pink' are flanked by a sweet bay magnolia. The Roses are particularly fond of the sweet bay and have more than twenty of them planted in their garden.

Here is another view of the Rose's garden cottage. Boston ivy covers the walls, hydrangea 'Nikko' flanks the stepping-stone pavement, and on the right, there is a white *Camellia japonica* high pruned as a tree, which offers a breathtaking bloom in early spring.

*Opposite:* This handsome old Victorian house is located in Shelter Island, New York. Designer Lisa Stamm has taken advantage of the shade that the canopy of large trees offers and has created a lush planting that isn't overheated. She has used hydrangea 'Nikko,' various hostas, ferns, and lavender daylilies.

*Above right:* Designer Jan Kirsh installed flower beds at Shery and Breene Kerr's property, Graycewood, near Easton, Maryland, located along the banks of the Tred Avon River. From the inside of the house, you can see the entire garden through the expanse of paned windows on the facade. In the foreground are clusters of blue, yellow, and white pansies, along with sweet woodruff, an herb that makes a fine ground cover, bearing white flowers in spring. The predominantly blue and white planting beside the river has a cooling effect.

*Below right:* Beside a charming little red barn at the Behnke-Dougherty country house in Southbury Connecticut, designer Wes Rouse planted pink cleome, sedum 'Autumn Joy,' and a collection of dwarf conifers, echoing the plantings at the main house (page 21). The flower colors blend harmoniously with the barn and the stone wall.

*Opposite:* Here is another view of Jan Kirsh's design at Graycewood near Easton, Maryland.

*Above:* An old schoolhouse, built around 1872 and moved to the Wines's farm in Jamesport, New York, from the nearby hamlet of Northville, has two doors, one for boys and one for girls. It's a perfect backdrop for Roger Wines's informal vegetable and cutting garden. In those days, it was counted a very good idea to separate the boys' entrance from the girls'. And quite probably, it would still be a good idea today.

Frank Cabot's lovely wall garden at Stonecrop in Garrison, New York, is surely one of the finest in America. Wall gardens have only recently become popular in the United States whereas in England, Ireland, and Scotland they have been familiar fixtures for more than a hundred years. Many plants thrive in the small cracks of the walls, including aubretia, sedum, echeveria, arabis, and saponaria.

STONE WALLS AND FENCES GIVE A GARDEN STRUCTURE. SHEDS, ARBORS, STATUARY, gazebos, gates, trellises, pergolas, and birdbaths are all finishing touches. Look around at yard sales and country auctions for these garden luxuries or search for abandoned farms or old houses that have sheds, outhouses, and so forth. Usually, the owners will be happy to give them to you. I did just that. Nearby were the abandoned remains of what was once a fine farm. There was a shed on the property that I felt would enhance my eighteenth-century house. My ninety-five-year-old neighbor, the granddaughter of the original owner, owned the place, and I asked if I could buy the shed and move it. She said, "It is not a shed, it was our carriage house, and it was built in 1812, the year Napoleon went to Russia! And I want to give it to you!" I gladly accepted, moved it, added a cupola and a weather vane, and it is today the most charming aspect of the property.

Charles and Barbara Robinson spent a considerable amount of time in the Far East. The pagoda-like structure, which they call the "folly," tucked into the small hillside at their garden in Washington, Connecticut, and built by Charles, reflects this influence. The planting is lavish, with canna lilies in the distance, sedum 'Autumn Joy,' and *Corydalis lutea*. And a mysterious woman seems to be emerging from the ancient stone wall.

*Opposite:* At Far-a-Field, John H. Whitworth's house in Millbrook, New York, one of the most beautiful gardens is a long, curving mixed border that is richly planted atop and beneath an old stone retaining wall. In the background you can see some bright blue delphiniums; lady's mantle is in the foreground. Ivy covers the wall, and plants are tucked into it wherever possible.

*Above:* A wonderful stone wall covered with climbing variegated euonymus at the Robinson's garden in Washington, Connecticut, looks as though it has been in place for centuries. Sedum 'Autumn Joy' is just starting to take on its summer pink color. Purple platycodon and phlox 'Bright Eyes' complete the planting. In the background is a rather fancy birdhouse, which was given to them by a friend.

*Opposite above:* Designer Paul Marchese created a lovely cottage garden bordered by an unusual picket fence at the Nisenson-Daniel country residence in East Dorset, Vermont. Paul tends to favor the old-fashioned perennials in his design schemes. Indeed, they are very appropriate for a Vermont country setting.

*Opposite below:* A charming cutting garden, filled with zinnias and enclosed by a white picket fence, welcomes visitors to the residence of Mr. and Mrs. Steven Lessing in Dorset, Vermont. More and more these days, cutting gardens have become standard in country gardens. They provide an endless supply of cut flowers for arrangements indoors.

*Below:* Conni Cross's design for the Isaac-Cosner garden in Cutchogue, New York, includes this enchanting courtyard with a lattice fence that lets the light in but still offers some privacy and protection from deer. The tall growing plants on the left include a white allium, a member of the onion family, often overlooked by gardeners.

This fence and gateway at the New Suffolk, New York, residence of Frederick and Sharon Koehler are softened with weeping Atlantic cedar. It's easy to train the tree to this shape. *Geranium sanguineum*, with its cerise blossoms, is on the left. In the foreground is heuchera 'Palace Purple,' grown for its stunning maroon foliage. *Corydalis lutea*, an easy-to-grow plant that self-seeds, is planted next to the heuchera.

Donna Wardlaw has created a wonderful
country garden in the backyard of her
house in Saratoga, New York. The wooden
fence helps to create a private little island
in the middle of the picturesque town.
*Clematis jackmanii* and the white spires
of cimicifuga dominate this planting,
along with feathery queen-of-the-prairie.

A tall border may add drama to a spectacular view. Here a perennial border of pink malva, yellow, orange, and red Asiatic lilies, and purple lupines and a handsome white fence frame the distant mountains in Pawlet, Vermont.

Ann and Charlie Yonkers's Pot Pie Farm was a working farm until as recently as 1970. Located on the Eastern Shore of Maryland, its spreading lawns and gardens are home to flocks of white doves. The fence that encloses the pool area is lavishly planted with all manner of summer-blooming annuals and perennials. Included in the planting are daylily 'Siloam Red Ruby,' fernleaf yarrow (Achillea filipendulina), some fuchsia-colored zinnias, and silvery artemisia.

Nancy Gilbert and Richard Wines of Jamesport, New York, cut these charming pickets on the fence that graces the front of one of their outbuildings with a table saw. The tulip motif derives from the nineteenth century. The bird on one of the pickets is an osprey, which was on the verge of extinction but now has flourished once again in the area and is off the endangered species list.

What a nice addition a planter filled with impatiens makes to this rather beautifully designed gate. Shade-loving hosta line the brick path. Designer Lisa Stamm often uses planters in all sorts of places in a garden and very effectively. Keep in mind that if planters are in direct sunlight, and during dry spells, they must be watered frequently or the plants will die.

John H. Whitworth has decorated the side of the garage at Far-a-Field, in Millbrook, New York, to near perfection. Trelliswork and the two large urns on either side of an espaliered pear tree support the yellow clematis 'Tangutika.'

Here's a little shed that Elizabeth Trammell of St. Michaels, Maryland, has dressed up with trelliswork. White and deep-pink phlox line the pathway. The main house is called "The Little House on Chestnut Street"; it's a bed and breakfast that can be rented by the day, week, or all summer. It is set on a lovely tree-lined street in the old part of town. Elizabeth has placed a fine old zinc watering can at the foot of the shed. You can find these at yard sales, along with other old garden implements to add charming touches to your property.

A few years ago, Harry Haralambou and I visited the garden of Madame de Belder outside of Brussels. We were out in the south forty when the rain started to come down in buckets and we had to take shelter in an open shed. The sound of the rain on the roof was unforgettable, and so the quest for a small outbuilding began. We found this outhouse on a playing field owned by the town where we live. The highway supervisor was glad to get rid of it so we moved it in pieces to the garden. Since there is a canopy of maples over the area, we opted for shade-loving plants. Various dwarf hostas, white impatiens, and red-and-green caladiums set off the building. The low-growing plant with the speckled leaves in the foreground is pulmonaria 'Mrs. Moon.'

*Left*: Another small outbuilding at the Robinson garden in Washington, Connecticut, is this tool shed, topped by a cupola and weather vane. The building is reminiscent of the Swiss chalet style, and the stone foundation, typical of farmhouses in Pennsylvania, reflects the fact that Charles Robinson originally hails from that part of the country. The chairs are from the public garden at Wave Hill in New York.

*Above*: The owner of this small outbuilding in Great Barrington, Massachusetts, uses it as a small guest cottage. Trumpet vines and morning glories that cover the structure add a romantic touch. A modest planting of annuals in front dresses it up and gives it a more substantial look. Without the plantings, this would be a dull building sitting in the middle of some grass.

41

*Below:* Designer Jan Kirsh of Bozman, Maryland, on the Eastern Shore, painted her small toolshed a bluish gray and installed blue fescue grass (*Festuca glauca* 'Elijah's Blue') close by, a fine complement to the lovely color of the outbuilding. *Hydrangea quercifolia* 'Snow Queen' and cherry laurel (*Prunus laurocerasus* 'Otto Luyken') flank the structure.

*Opposite above:* This charming outbuilding, set on a spreading green lawn, is in Dorset, Vermont, and is seen from the roadside. In the foreground are bright orange wild tiger lilies, ubiquitous throughout the eastern part of the United States. The owner has planted white Shasta daisies and yellow coreopsis in front of the house in sharp contrast to the somber colors of the house facade.

*Opposite below:* Here's a small outbuilding along the side of a country road in Great Barrington, Massachusetts, in the heart of the Berkshires. The owner has dressed up this old shed with a planting of white flowers. Nicotiana, cleome, and cosmos are set off by silver foliaged plants. The window boxes are made of old barn siding, in keeping with the facade of the outbuilding.

*Left:* Designer Lisa Stamm fills gray pots with brilliant red verbena and donkey tails (*Sedum morganianum*) The verbena is a nice change from more predictable red geraniums.

*Opposite:* Deep in the woods of the Berkshire Mountains in Massachusetts is this rustic country getaway. A tub of impatiens in the lawn makes a moveable flower bed. The "window" on the facade is actually a mirror, in this simple but clever garden designed by Laura Lee Walton.

One of the signatures of landscape designer Wes Rouse is to use container plantings worked in with traditional perennial and annual borders. This stunning combination of the tender grass *Pennisetum rubrum* and *Petunia integrefolia* graces and softens the fieldstone wall at the foreground of the photograph. White nicotiana 'Nikki' is seen at the right.

See what you can do with a simple stone staircase? At their Garrison, New York, garden, Gerald and Carol Prueitt have decorated every step of this one with terra-cotta pots of annuals, including nasturtiums and petunias, sweet alyssums, and calendulas.

Designer Conni Cross adds yard-sale finds to her landscape designs. Here an old zinc washtub serves as a planter for trailing lobelia and brilliant crimson pelargoniums, commonly, and mistakenly, called geraniums. In the background is a Japanese maple, *Acer palmatum* 'Bloodgood.' In the foreground are various varieties of epimedium.

As you stroll through small country towns, you'll see many old houses with elaborate container-plant arrangements and hanging baskets on the porches. This fine old tradition, so much a part of Americana, has largely vanished from ever-spreading suburban environments. I guess suburban folks don't like to sit on the porch and gossip.

Helga and Charlie Michel have decorated their porch with containers of white impatiens, which thrive in the shade of the overhanging roof, and hanging baskets of scarlet ivy geraniums. The broom is always nearby. Since it is an old-fashioned straw broom, it adds a rather charming touch to the scene, doesn't it? You see! There's nothing wrong with leaving a nice broom on the porch.

Here's our laburnum walk. We call it that
despite the fact that famous gardener
Robert Dash of Sagaponac, New York,
says that our sixteen-foot walk is not long
enough to be called a walk and is instead
an arbor. The statue of the putto is a
recent addition. Some of our grand
friends insist that we call him Wolfgang.
We have settled for "Butch." A laburnum
walk is made up of laburnum trees that
have been trained to grace an arbor. This
one blooms spectacularly in May and is
my favorite display of all in the garden.

*Opposite:* A weathered old garden bench is flanked by two large containers planted with Boston fern (*Nephrolepsis exaltata* 'Bostoniensis') in a quiet part of the Rose's garden in St. Michaels, Maryland. This tender houseplant is brought indoors during the winter.

*Above left:* An elegant Victorian planter filled with purple petunias adds a nice touch to the patio at Wheelbarrow Hill Farm in Great Barrington, Massachusetts, owned by Richard and Candace K. Beinecke. Laura Lee Walton designed the garden.

*Above right:* At Peg and Bob Keller's Bolton Farm on Maryland's Eastern Shore, a fine antique marble pedestal stands in a niche in a wall. A red goldflame honeysuckle *(Lonicera* X *heckrottii)* rambles around the lovely old ornament, filling the air with its unforgettable fragrance.

# Country Seats

USED TO BE, DOWN SOUTH, THAT PORCHES WERE USED FOR DRINKIN' MASH AND talkin' trash. With the changes in architectural style during the latter part of this century, porches have largely disappeared. In their place are patios. If you have an old house, you are probably blessed with a fine porch, a place to decorate with lavish hanging plant baskets, rocking chairs, and beautiful people. Today's American patio, largely a twentieth-century creation, serves the same purpose. If you have a choice, locate your patio close to the house since carrying trays back and forth from the kitchen will be a daily ritual. My late father always said, "Never go back to the house empty-handed." Whether for solitary relaxation, convivial visiting, hard-nosed gossip, or serious drinking, porches and patios remain essential to country living.

*Opposite:* One of the water gardens at designer Conni Cross's Cutchogue, New York, garden is a showplace of shade-loving plants: a lavish planting of columbines, azaleas, campanulas, narcissus, and pulmonaria, along with hosta and several dwarf conifers. I can't think of a better place to curl up with a good book and forget about everything else.

*Right:* How about it? Time for a snooze? Cross chose this secluded part of her property for the hammock and playhouse. Note the blue bench in the distance. A bit of off beat color in the garden adds visual interest.

*Left:* I don't expect there could be a more inviting porch anywhere than this one in Saratoga, New York, belonging to Charles and Candice Wait. The potted palm gives the porch an extravagant, tropical look. Saratoga is famous for its porches, and homeowners in town often create elaborate displays of potted plants and hanging baskets.

*Below left:* At Barnsley House in England, Rosemary Verey found a nineteenth-century reproduction of a Greek temple, which she moved to her famous garden creating a shady retreat. To set it off, she installed a small pond with water lilies and various irises. Take a page from her book and look around for small structures that you might be able to move to your garden.

*Opposite:* Here is another porch, this one in Great Barrington, Massachusetts. It's a perfect place to sit and rock and enjoy an ice-cold lemonade, a dish of homemade ice cream, or a double bourbon with a beer chaser, if need be.

*Opposite:* One expects to see an Odalisque sensuously reclined on the sofa inside this wonderfully eccentric folly at Lisa Stamm and Dale Booher's garden in Shelter Island, New York. In front of the folly is a down-to-earth, honest-to-God barbecue pit.

*Right:* Notice the cutout of iris and daffodils on the back wall of this charming, latticed shelter built by Charles Robinson in Washington, Connecticut. The cutout is backed with stained glass, and in the evening when the sun sets it glows with the rich color of the glass, certainly one of the loveliest innovations we've seen in our travels.

*Left:* Wrought-iron furniture goes with the nineteenth-century wrought-iron gate in the Rose's garden in St. Michaels, Maryland. The water garden is planted with lotus and water lilies. The plantings include dependable hostas and Japanese maples.

A house in Great Barrington, Massachusetts, sits high up on a hill, with gardens leading down to the banks of this lovely river. The owners hung a loveseat from a bankside tree. As you swing, you go back and forth over the riverbank and over the water, a delightful experience and one simple to have for yourself, if you are fortunate enough to live along a country stream.

*Right:* What could be more of a tranquil hideaway than landscape designer DeeDee Finkelstein's woodland water garden in Remsenberg, New York. The spectacular, cerise-colored shrub in the background is rhododendron 'Cynthia.' At the foot of the classic rustic bench is a planting of Japanese primroses.

*Left:* Randy and Dot Rose's garden in St. Michaels, Maryland, contains room after room of enchantment. Here is a reflecting pool, planted with hardy lotus and water lilies, with four cherubs, symbolizing the four seasons, at the corners. The Roses built the trellis screen themselves, using posts made from a stand of juniper trees on the property. The seat in front of it is a bit more formal than most: only dignified conversation is allowed here.

*Above:* This small courtyard garden outside of Brussels, Belgium, is certainly one of the most beautiful that we have ever seen. The terra-cotta pots are filled with hydrangeas, ivy, hostas, and several with dwarf conifers. Purple benches are not to everyone's taste, but you must admit that this one is just the thing.

A lot of inexperienced gardeners throw up their hands in despair when confronted with an area in their garden that is deeply shaded. Take a look at our shade garden. A fine old bench looks over shade-loving tuberous begonias ('cut and come again'), caladiums, hosta, coneflowers, and lamium. It's a perfect place to take a snooze or do whatever else one does in a secluded shade garden.

*Right:* Just look at how these container plantings of pansies and gerbera welcome visitors to the residence of Mr. and Mrs. Robert Ferguson of Dorset, Vermont. A hanging basket of ivy and Molly, the family pet, help.

Designer Conni Cross of Cutchogue, New York, has surrounded her porch with a planting of dwarf conifers and flowering shrubs. What a lovely place for lunch. The stunning lavender azalea on the right is 'Kurume Skikibu.' In the background is the white dogwood 'Cloud Nine.' The yellow heather in the foreground is 'Gold Haze.'

63

# Whimsy in the Garden

A GARDEN IS A PLACE FOR RELAXATION, CONTEMPLATION, AND FUN. AND THUS, throughout garden history, captivating touches of whimsy were added to entertain, surprise, and enchant visitors. I'm not referring to tacky concrete rabbits, screaming pink flamingos, or cutouts of grotesque dwarfs. During the eighteenth century, plumbing systems were installed beneath paved courtyards at many European chateaus and palaces: When visitors stepped on certain stones, small fountains would suddenly, but gently, gush water, sending visitors fleeing from the spot to avoid getting wet. Today we don't hose down our guests, but you can add whimsical touches such as mirrors on fences and walls, hidden gardens, and vine-covered statues to surprise visitors. On a grander scale, we've seen pet peacocks, a deer park, a collection of enormous mill wheels, and, in lieu of James Thurber's mythical unicorn, a pet pig named Henrietta that wandered willy-nilly through the petunia patches at a garden we visited in Millbrook, New York.

*Opposite:* In this amusing corner of William and Barbara Tyree's garden in Cutchogue, New York, which was designed by Conni Cross, two Victorian ladies and a handsome German shepherd pose eternally for passersby. The garden in the background is planted with gooseneck loosestrife.

*Left:* Gwynn Hubbell of Millbrook, New York, has a charming small farm on a lovely country lane. Along with a cat, three dogs, a rooster, and a herd of Welsh ponies, which she breeds, is a surprise pet. Believe it or not, Henrietta sticks to the paths and does not tramp around in the garden.

Sculptor Toni Putnam chose to use her garden in Garrison, New York, as a showcase for some of her art. The curved wall and plantings of coneflower, lavender, coreopsis, and other perennials provide a lovely setting for her metal sculptures.

At the Robinson garden in Washington, Connecticut, Charles Robinson added this architecturally unique archway, replete with a hanging basket of akebia and container-grown plants. The steps in front of the archway are old curb-stones rescued from the streets of Hartford, Connecticut. Through the woods is Charles's water garden. His wife, Barbara, calls it his waterworks, for there are fourteen different pools descending from the top of the hill.

*Left:* In a wild, overgrown section of the garden at the Stamm-Booher house in Shelter Island, New York, Lisa has added a pair of weathered columns. The Victorians had a romantic preoccupation with ruins in the garden. If you decide to add a ruin of some sort to your garden, the best place to find it is a junk-yard or a place that sells old architectural detail material. Whatever you do, don't go out and spend a fortune for white vinyl columns because that's exactly what they end up looking like, white vinyl columns. Awful.

*Right:* At landscape designer Wes Rouse's garden in Southbury, Connecticut, traditional garden sculptures of the four seasons look out over a lush green lawn. Naturally, since Wes is a designer, he has a greenhouse on his prop-erty, where he grows all manner of tropical and sub-tropical plants in tubs and large pots. He incor-porates these into his landscape schemes during the spring and summer. The flowering small tree in the middle is coprosma, a tropical plant from New Zealand.

*Opposite:* Certainly beyond the reach of almost all gardeners is the deer park at the Clark residence in Millbrook, New York. From the rear of the country house you can spot this Greek temple perched high up on a distant hill, where a very large, fenced-in deer park is home to about one hundred deer. I asked the owner if this was perhaps the last deer park left in America. Deer parks were quite popular during the late nineteenth and early twentieth centuries. He said he thought it was. My only comment was, "Hmm, you people don't mess around, do you?"

*Below:* Designer Lisa Stamm installed these wooden swans on either side of a small flight of steps in an East Hampton, New York, garden. Clouds of snow-in-summer flank the staircase, giving it an old-fashioned look.

*Left:* Marcia Donahue of Berkeley, California, is an artist who chooses to express her creativity in the garden as well as in her art. Her whimsical touches, some amusing, some bizarre, are seen throughout the garden. Here a primitive stone mask is sunken just below water level in a pond, smirking at passersby. Shock and surprises. The plant material in the garden is a strange combination: traditional roses and tropical plants that, surprisingly enough, go rather well together.

Artist Arthur Jones of Dorset, Vermont, has converted an enormous barn into a magnificent country house. Tucked in here and there are macabre touches, like this strange mask peering out of a planting of sedums and mosses.

*Right:* Sonny Garcia's intimate garden in San Francisco includes this walkway, which is paved with some of Marcia Donahue's whimsical carved stone masks. Notice how he uses plants that complement the colors of the sculptures, such as burgundy ajuga, black mondo grass, and green thyme.

Lisa Stamm designed this garden in Shelter Island, New York, containing the property with a long trellis fence. She opted not to paint it white but a subtle greenish blue. Keep that in mind when you make structural additions to your garden. White is not always the right color because it can dominate and even overburden a landscape. Notice that she created an oval frame with a stone obelisk behind it. This provides an illusion that the garden goes on and on. Mirrors in the right places can be used for similar effect.

*Left:* Here at her own residence near Easton, Maryland, Jan Kirsh has installed a unique treatment for the foundation. There is no cliche planting of dwarf conifers here. She has opted to echo the cobblestone path pattern with a random use of cobblestones interplanted with low growing plants, right along the foundation of the house.

Mary-Jane Emmet, of West Stockbridge, Massachusetts, has a long, very green dwarf conifer border leading up to her house. "Why not plant pumpkins?" she mused one day. The foliage is lush, large, and dramatic; the plant grows vigorously and fills in the empty spaces; and the pumpkins add a wonderfully whimsical touch and brilliant color to the border in early fall.

A mirror stragetically placed on a wall can create interesting visual juxtapositions. Here the windowbox planting goes perfectly with the border in the distance.

# Water Gardens and Pools

Y OU CAN IMAGINE OUR UNBOUNDED EXCITEMENT THE FIRST TIME WE TURNED ON the pump in our water garden and water gently cascaded down the three levels of our new waterfall and into the pond. As always in the country, word got around, and soon generous friends brought snails, water lilies, parrot feathers, lotus, goldfish, and fantails. One friend offered a koi that had outgrown his fish tank. For amusement, I added smoked salmon and filet of sole. Soon rare songbirds discovered it and came to splash in the water. Perhaps you've wondered where the fish spend the winter? I did, and worried about it. Well, they retreat to the deepest part of the pond and head for the wet bar, where they drink all winter, coming up for air in spring. Here are some lovely water gardens that we hope will give you some ideas.

*Opposite:* The H.B. Atwater residence in Dorset, Vermont, is blessed with a fine small waterfall and gently meandering stream. Designer Paul Marchese used it to full advantage in designing the landscape. He opted for a natural look, a minimum of colorful flowers, and one fine Victorian wrought-iron bench as a focal point on the lush green lawn.

*Right:* During the summer, this Long Island garden, designed by Sanford Kempner, becomes a cooling symphony in green. The manmade stream is planted with dwarf deutzia, ajuga 'Burgundy Glow,' variegated ginger, climbing hydrangea, and a split-leaf maple.

*Opposite left:* Designer Paul Marchese of Dorset, Vermont, landscaped this charming old country house, which belongs to Mr. and Mrs. Robert Ferguson. The stream ran right through the back of the property and was lined with native plants. Paul added some stones here and there and flowers, including many that thrive in a marshy environment. Included in the plantings are bog-loving Japanese iris, pink monarda 'Croftway,' white astilbe, and common orange tiger lilies.

*Opposite right:* When Pat Lisciandro bought her country house in Dorset, Vermont, she was blessed with a small brook running through the back of the property. She decided to give it the appearance of a mountain stream, using large rocks. Included in the planting are white Shasta daisies, pink balloon flowers, yellow yarrow, malva, blue nepeta, and white phlox.

*Left:* This meandering stream, which looks so natural, was installed by designer Sanford Kempner and operates by a pump. The plantings include white impatiens, coleus 'Penny,' the popular grass pennisetum 'Hamlin,' and, in the stream, watercress, which can be picked and used to make preposterous little sandwiches or a chilled soup for a summer lunch.

A pond is enlivened by yellow flag iris, lythrum 'Robert,' various hostas, and a small toy sail boat. The design is by Conni Cross.

*Opposite:* A gravel path winds its away around the water garden designed by Conni Cross for Maurice Isaac and Ellen Coster of Cutchogue, New York. The dwarf conifer on the left is a false cypress (*Chamaecyparis obtusa* 'Nana'). The red Japanese maple is *Acer palmatum* var. *dissectum* 'Crimson Queen.' Blue-and-white Japanese irises, forget-me-nots, and sedum 'Kamtschaticum' offer color and texture to the waterside garden.

*Above:* Nelly the pup, a shepherd mix, feels right at home in another view of the same garden. Pondside are pale lavender Japanese irises, hosta 'Sun and Substance,' *Miscanthus sinensis, Styrax japonicus pendula,* lythrum 'Morden's Pink," and hydrangea 'Tardiva.'

At the end of April, yellow and blue are the primary colors of our water garden, designed by Ken Ruzicka, thanks to mini-daffodils, blue *Phlox subulata*, and blue anemones. The ponds fed by the waterfalls are stocked with koi and planted with water lilies and lotus. Both fish and plants survive cold winters if the pond is deep enough. This one is four feet deep at one end. Plants are placed in the deep area, and fish and frogs winter there.

*Opposite:* Many plants have been hybridized at Allen Bloom's splendid estate in Bressingham, England, with its magnificent water garden. Bloom has been in the plant business for many many years, sports long white hair, and wears an earring. Our good friend Lady Scott, also known as Valerie Finnis, of Dower House in Northamptonshire says that despite his long hair and the earring, he's not that sort!

No matter how modest a water garden is, the gurgling sound of water adds a wonderful quality of life to any garden. Here a simple trough, with a spigot and one aquatic umbrella plant, makes a water garden in a shady corner of designer Lisa Stamm and Dale Booher's garden.

This is Arthur Ross's water garden at his country house in Garrison, New York. Water lilies and various foliage water plants grow in the water and goldfish and frogs live here. Gravel lines the waterside, and several large stones provide a place to relax and enjoy the sounds and sights of the garden. Ross, however, does not confine his love of water in the garden to the pond. He recently installed a thirty-foot-high waterfall. Now that's a big waterfall. That's a very big waterfall.

Mrs. and Mrs. Robert C.A. Brantjes of Garrison, New York, opted for a green look in the landscape surrounding their natural-looking swimming pool. Dwarf conifers such as mugo pine, Alberta spruce, and several Colorado spruce trees adorn the pool banks. Normally, Colorado spruces will grow to more than fifty feet, but by annual pruning and shearing the Brantjes have kept the tree within bounds.

*Opposite:* Here's a swimming pool that looks like the "ole swimmin' hole" of yore, designed by Conni Cross. Dwarf conifers in the background include *Cedrus deodara* 'Aurea Pendula' and *Pinus parviflora* 'Glauca Nana.' Conni uses lantana 'Confetti' and weeping purple lantana for touches of color around the pool.

*Right:* The stunning view of the Berkshire foothills from designer Peter Dunlop's swimming pool is breathtaking. The only pool view that I've seen that approaches it in beauty is at the legendary Hôtel du Cap in Antibes in the south of France, which is carved out of the rocks and perched high above the bluffs overlooking the Mediterranean Sea. At the Hôtel du Cap, the haunting scent of mimosa fills the air. In the Berkshires, Peter has graced his pool with a series of white cylindrical containers, all planted with bright yellow marigolds and crimson geraniums.

Designer Sanford Kempner has surrounded this formal swimming pool with unusual annuals. The lovely lavender verbena 'Bonariensis' and helix 'Cream and Green' fill classic terra-cotta containers. *Petunia integrefolia*, white cleome, portulaca, and pink zinnias brighten up the background.

*Opposite*: The late distinguished interior designer, Jean Patrice Coutraud, also known as the Duc de Bourbon-Paris, had a flair for combining simplicity and elegance. As a result, his conceptions were always unpretentious and warm. This small outbuilding glows with a light inside, and the sparse furnishings

offer an easy elegance. Notice that he chose to paint the pool lining a very dark blue-black rather than the ubiquitous aqua. It is a unique touch, a startling departure from the conventional, for the pool more resembles a reflecting pool in a formal garden than a swimming pool.

Like newly fallen snow, sweet-smelling, late summer blooming sweet autumn clematis drapes the pergola that adjoins the pool and frames the distant statue in an East Hampton, New York, garden designed by Mary Beth Lee.

Artists Margaret Kerr and Robert Richenburg 's medieval herb garden, which surrounds their formal fishpond, is planted with scores of herbs and cultivars authentic to the period. In the foreground, a fine stand of lavender and feverfew.

# Vegetable Gardens

Truman capote once said that the difference between the rich and the rest of us is that the rich eat very tiny vegetables: peas the size of BBs, baby beets, baby carrots, baby limas. If you grow your own vegetables, you can enjoy these elegant morsels regularly. And then there are tomatoes. There is nothing quite like a warm, sun-drenched tomato picked and eaten right off the vine. The resident pooch here, an apricot cockapoo named Mr. Chips, like the rich, is a devotee of tiny cherry tomatoes. In fact, when guests are here, he picks one for each and sets it down in front of him or her. Needless to say, this gesture of generosity endears him to all, even our rich friends.

*Opposite:* Certainly one of the most stunning potagers in the garden world is that of Rosemary Verey at Barnsley House in the Cotswold countryside of England. Here she grows marrows, which the British call squash, on an arbor, with the vegetables listlessly hanging over a bed of nasturtiums.

*Left:* The Roses of St. Michaels, Maryland, use raised beds for their vegetable garden along with a gravel ground cover. This simplifies weeding, watering, and fertilizing. The bamboo A-frame serves as a support for vigorous pole beans, making them not only easy to care for but easy to pick as well.

This charming little cottage at Jane Treman Gilbert's Dorset, Vermont, house serves as her husband Clinton's office. While he conducts business he can sit and look out over the tomato patch. A sprinkler system was installed to ease maintenance. Note that here and there French marigolds are planted. These serve as natural repellents for many pesky insects. Garlic is another plant that repels insects.

*Right:* A vegetable garden is the perfect complement to the Wines's collection of old buildings in Jamesport, New York. For years, they have been buying farm out-buildings, moving them to their property, and restoring them. This barn is called the Corwin-Hallock Barn and was originally built by Richard's great-great-great-great-grandfather at the end of the eighteenth century.

*Left:* Another view of Jane Treman Gilbert's garden with the Taconic Mountains in the distance. It is enclosed by a six-foot-high deer fence, the beds are all raised for easy maintenance, and wood chips keep the weeds down in the pathways. Summer squash, scallions, tomatoes, oakleaf lettuce, and other vegetables provide fresh food for the table.

*Below left:* Mr. and Mrs. Robert Ferguson of Dorset, Vermont, have a vegetable garden that anyone could be proud of.

*Opposite:* While driving out of Manchester, Vermont, we spotted this fine vegetable garden graced with two rather jolly scarecrows. Yes, they do scare the crows away. At least, a little bit, anyway. A part of the American country tradition, scarecrows add whimsical touches to almost all vegetable gardens. In some parts of the country, there are competitions held each year with prizes given for the most attractive and original scarecrows.

*Opposite:* This immaculately maintained potager at Mr. and Mrs. John Whitmore's Langdon Farm in Sherwood, Maryland, is designed so that the texture and colors of the vegetable foliage complement and enhance each other. A potager is a vegetable garden that, like a flower garden, is a thing of beauty, not just row upon row of vegetables. Here the unlikely combination of red cabbage, onions, and beets planted in front of a bed of roses is simply beautiful. Beds of lavender and Shasta daisies are close by, with bright yellow French marigolds serving as insect repellents.

*Above:* Nancy Shwindt grows lettuce, squash, string beans, broccoli, basil, tomatoes, and other vegetables for the table. A planting of red bee balm, an old-fashioned flower, adjoins the barn. Its leaves, when dried, make a fine tea, sometimes called Oswego tea. It is, incidentally, the secret ingredient in Earl Gray tea, which gives it its distinctive taste.

*Left:* Don't miss out on the glorious experience of growing and eating your own vegetables. It is a very gratifying endeavor. The owner of this garden in Great Barrington, Massachusetts, has a ready supply of food for dinner right smack in his own backyard.

On the East End of Long Island, the days of potato farming are numbered. There is no money in potatoes anymore. The same has been said about lima beans for more than hundred years. These days, the farmers have switched to growing sod, nursery stock (as seen here), and vinifera grapes, which are made into superb wines that now win medals in competition with California and French wines. We say that the environment has been saved by the bottle.

# Country Gardening: A Brief Practical Guide

THE INFORMATION PROVIDED IN THIS section of the book will get you off to a flying start with your country garden. It is written for inexperienced gardeners. Obviously, you are interested in creating a beautiful garden at your country house or you wouldn't be reading this book right now. While you read, let your mind wander and begin to get some idea of what you might want to do with your landscape.

Before you start to dream, however, heed some advice. Gardening should be a gratifying, creative, and relaxing pursuit. After all, you probably bought a country house to get away from the stress of daily business and city or suburban living. In other words, you are getting back to nature and into a casual, informal mode. Don't lay a heavy gardening number on yourself. Keep your garden a manageable size; if you overextend yourself, the entire purpose of creating a tranquil and beautiful garden, that is, a place to escape from daily cares, will be lost.

One of the most important lessons that gardening teaches is patience. Many of us are accustomed to having exactly what we want when we want it. But when you are dealing with nature, you have no control over your garden beyond a certain point. It is a humbling experience.

Remember that good gardening practice is a combination of experience and information. Don't be discouraged by lack of either, for both are attainable. Read books, talk to people, get advice, visit public gardens and nurseries, and get out there and dig. Further, don't be afraid to be adventurous. For whatever reason, Americans seem to be very reticent about trying something new in the garden, and that includes experienced gardeners as well as novices.

Don't worry about what your mother-in-law thinks about your garden. Don't worry about what your friends think about your garden. Learn from everyone, including me, and then do pretty much what you want to do. You are gardening for yourself and for your family. This is the way to learn. You will make mistakes and you will have triumphs, and you will be paving the pathway to wisdom.

## First Things First: Accessing the Site

As a gardener, you want to know what plants will survive and thrive in your garden. To answer this question, you must be familiar with the general climate, weather, soil, and moisture conditions in your area. In general, climate is a constant, while weather, soil, and water conditions may change dramatically from place to place.

The Agricultural Research Service of the U.S. Department of Agriculture has divided the United States into eleven plant hardiness zones for the convenience of gardeners and farmers. These zones are determined by average annual minimum temperature. You will frequently see these zones mentioned in garden catalogues and books. The map is widely disseminated. Some web sites, such as Virtual Garden (www.vg.com), will tell you your zone if you type in your zip code. Occasionally plants will thrive in your garden that allegedly can't be grown at that latitude. I have had great success in growing camellias, which usually have to winter under glass this far north, in my Eastern Long Island garden, with the oldest, a sixteen-foot-tall pink *Camellia japonica* now in its twenty-first year.

### Planning Considerations

• Plan your design taking seasonal changes into account. Let's say you have a detached garage and that some of the ground between it and your house is subject to flooding in late winter or spring. If you install a path in the wrong place, you might end up having to walk through six inches of water every time you need your car in certain months.

• In situating your outdoor living area, think of convenience to the kitchen since chances are when you entertain you will be going back and forth with food and drinks for your guests or for yourself. If you have children, place their play area—swings, seesaws, sandboxes—where you can watch them conveniently through a window in the kitchen or other part of the house.

• Plan your vegetable garden so that it is also near the kitchen. My first vegetable garden was way back in the rear of my property. Often when cooking, I'd omit herbs that were too far away because it wasn't worth stopping what I was doing to gather them. Eventually, I woke up and put a modest vegetable and herb garden right next to the kitchen door.

• Plan with your pets in mind. If you have a dog, find out if there's a leash law in your area. If so, it is best to abide by it for the sake of good neighborly relations. If there is and your dog has not been trained to remain on your property, you have several options. You can take him for walks, build a dog run, chain him, or become well acquainted with the local dogcatcher.

• You'll need a place to keep garbage until it's picked up. I recommend building or buying a small wooden compartment for the cans. It can be painted, and flowers or shrubs can be planted in front of it to dress it up. It should be secure enough so that animals cannot get into it. Put it as close as possible to the kitchen or rear entrance of the house.

If you have just bought your country house or if you are just beginning to landscape it, the first year of your landscape project should be spent getting to know your land—that is, identifying established plantings you already have; deciding what your needs are and what you wish to make of the property; and deciding which existing structures, such as patios, paths, or steps, are properly located for your needs. If, for example, you move into your house in the fall, you will have absolutely no idea whether or not there are any spring bulbs, such as daffodils or tulips, on the property. Perennial plantings will be scruffy, usually going into dormancy. Spring-blooming shrubs will be cloaked in autumn foliage with no flowers. Only in the spring, when things begin to grow and flowers and flowering shrubs and trees bloom, will you begin to see what you have.

Recruit a knowledgeable friend to identify plants and take notes as you walk around together assessing your land. A gardener's best friend is a dated notebook. Each year you can record your observations on the appropriate date. Write down anything that might help you later on in designing or redesigning your landscape. Date of bloom for individual plants is especially important: this is easy to forget from one year to another.

## Selecting Trees and Shrubs

Trees and shrubs are the backbone of any garden. If you want to have a garden, the first question to ask yourself when you survey your property is how much you need to change in the way of major plantings and how much of what is already there you can and want to live with.

Unless you have a really clear idea of what you want to do, leave the existing trees and shrubs alone for a season and see what they're like. Often there is a reason why they are there in the first place. They may have been

Pear

planted for shade, as a windscreen, or for privacy. Remember also that many trees grow no faster than you do. If you have a hillside on your property with a fine stand of shade trees and conifers, consider that it would take a generation to replace them should you cut them down.

There are many uses for trees and shrubs. They can be used as single specimens to provide focal points in the garden, in foundation plantings, as windbreaks, as plantings to control erosion, to provide shade, in shrub borders or hedges for privacy, and to divide one area of your property from another. For windbreaks, people generally rely on a few tough coniferous species. Privacy barriers are also usually composed of evergreens (unless you want to become an exhibitionist in the winter). If you want a hedge effect rather than an informal look, choose a broad-leaved evergreen with small leaves, such as holly. These can be kept to the desired height and width by

## Foundation Plantings

• As a rule, in the Northern Hemisphere, deciduous trees are best planted on southern, eastern, or western exposures–those parts of the house that face south east or west–because their leaves shade the house during the hot days of summer, providing nature's own air conditioning. During winter, these same trees lose their leaves and permit sun to filter into the house, providing a certain amount of heat.

• Evergreens are best planted on the northern exposure–the part of the house that faces north–for they retain their leaves in winter and provide insulation from cold and wind to that portion of the house. If prevailing winds in your area are from the west, and in most parts of the country they are, evergreens will serve as a windbreak if planted on the western exposure.

• An all-dwarf conifer foundation planting is very boring in that it includes little or no variety in color and texture. At the same time, a planting of only deciduous shrubs will look barren and ugly during the winter. The best way to approach this planting is to consider the texture of foliage, the color of the foliage in different seasons, the color of the blossoms, and the ultimate height of the plant and then select from the three types of shrubs: dwarf conifers, broad-leaved evergreens, and deciduous plants. Once you've decided which plants you want to use, design your scheme in an informal manner. Remember that you are in the country: in rural areas formal shrub plantings are quite out of place. In general, avoid making your planting symmetrical.

• Vary the height of the planting. Although it would seem only common sense to take note of windows when planning a foundation planting, many people neglect to do so. Do not place tall shrubs in front of windows for they will block the view outside and prevent sunlight from shining into the house. (By the same token, plan your flower borders so that you can see them through your windows.) Avoid shrubs that overgrow their bounds and would impede

*Continued on page 106*

*Continued from page 105*
passage to and from the house. Further, avoid plantings shrubs with thorns or climbing rosebushes close to the entrance of the house.

• When installing a foundation planting, do not, under any circumstance, select standard-sized conifers for your planting. Although they will be of manageable size when you purchase them, a few years down the line they will outgrow the planting, requiring expensive removal. Consider that a Norway spruce may be only four feet high when you install it, but then after a few years it can tower to more than forty or fifty feet.

• Avoid installing a foundation planting in a straight line. Space some plants close to the foundation and others farther out. In other words, create a garden in front of your house in much the same way that you would plant a perennial border.

• If you are selecting from small, low-growing plants, consider planting three of each variety together in one area rather than one of three different varieties. This will tie the planting together and give it a unified appearance.

• Perhaps most important, allow enough space to accommodate the mature size of the plants. Even the most experienced gardeners often make this mistake. If you do not, in a few short years the foundation planting will look overcrowded and overgrown and may even have to be yanked out and replaced. If you have installed your planting properly, it should look just a bit sparse for the first year or two. In a few years, the planting will fill out and be appropriate for the landscape.

• Finally, once you've installed your foundation planting, dress it up with an assortment of spring-blooming bulbs, perennials, and annuals.

annual trimming. Imaginative gardeners have made hedges out of many curious plants, but traditional hedging species are dense shrubs that take pruning well. If you decide that you wish to soften the formal effect of a screen, you can install deciduous shrubs and dwarf conifers as well as perennials, annuals, and spring-blooming bulbs in front of it. If a less formal shrub border is what you have in mind, select from all three categories: flowering deciduous shrubs, flowering broad-leaved evergreens, and dwarf conifers. When you design your border, keep in mind that the deciduous shrubs will lose their leaves in the winter, so space the evergreen varieties you select throughout the planting so the border will not look spotty during the winter. Deciduous trees, and particularly varieties with beautiful flowers or fruits, are customarily used to provide shade or as ornamental specimens (but be careful not to situate trees that will drop flowers or fruits on or next to patios).

Never select a shrub, or any plant, for that matter, simply because you happen to like the color of its flowers. Consider all of its aspects—shape, height, growth, habit, and foliage—and be sure it is in keeping with the scheme you have in mind.

## Perennials

If shrubs, hedges, and trees are the backbone of the landscape, certainly perennial flowering plants are the backbone of a country flower garden. They are long-lasting and winter hardy, that is, each fall their stalks wither and die, only to grow again from the roots, or crown, the following spring. You will see them referred to as "herbaceous" plants, which means that, unlike shrubs and trees, they have almost no woody tissue that survives from season to season. While you do not have to start with new plants each spring, as you do with annuals, perennials tend to bloom for a shorter span of time, some in late spring, some in summer, and some in fall.

Perennials can be used in many different ways in a garden. Ambitious gardeners group them together in borders (if they form strips between a walk or lawn and a wall) or island beds (if they are open on all sides). This can be complicated because you must try to achieve a harmonious blend of colors and forms that change throughout the spring, summer, and fall. Always think about the color, texture, and shape of the foliage when you select perennials. If a certain cultivar sports a beautiful flower but its foliage is problematical or ugly, avoid it. Remember that a plant without flowers in May provides green, silvery, gray, or blue foliage and thus provides color even though not in bloom. Some perennials are evergreen and add interest to your border or bed during winter months. Try to plan your scheme so that there is something in bloom from spring to fall.

Perennials also can be used to brighten the landscape after spring-blooming bulbs have finished, to add color to monotonous foundation plantings, to brighten driveways and paths, to accent garden structures, and for splashes of color in distant parts of the garden. Plant large groups of each variety for the best visual results. Do not plant symmetrically; rather, try to emulate nature and plant informally. Certain perennial plants are used as ground covers because they have handsome foliage and a low-growing spreading habit that makes them useful alternatives to that universal ground cover, the lawn.

The perennial cultivars that I have included in the "Plant Lists" (beginning on page 135) adapt well to a country garden and are generally readily available. They are, to a great extent, pest and disease free. Most of the cultivars that are listed under "Grasses," "Herbs," and "Vines" in the lists are perennials since they are hardy and bear new flowers every year, and as you see from the photographs in

## Designing Flower Beds

- You might want to try both a border and an island bed to decide which is best for your property. Keep in mind that a border, in order to be effective, should be at least six feet deep if you plan on using tall-growing plants as well as shorter varieties. However, if you wish to limit yourself to plants that are about one and a half feet high, a three- or four-foot border will be suitable. Free-form island beds containing taller-growing varieties should be about eight feet across at their widest point. The bed should be about three times as long as it is wide. If you wish to install medium-height and low-growing plants, a five-or six-foot-wide island bed is suitable.

- Don't let yourself get hung up about using only perennials for your beds. It is very difficult to create effective summer-long flower plantings using only perennials.

- In a border, place tall

*Continued on page 108*

Poppies and heliopsis

*Continued from page 107*

plants in the rear, medium-height plants in the middle, and low-growing varieties in front. In an island bed, taller plants go in the middle, surrounded by medium-height plants, with low-growing plants around the edge.

• Always think in terms of color combinations rather than individual varieties. Try to blend colors pleasingly, avoiding clashing combinations. Combinations such as screaming orange, brilliant red, and sulfur yellow are very difficult to use harmoniously. If you are familiar with a color wheel, you know that continuous segments are the most harmonious: for example, red, red-violet, and violet; blue, blue-violet, and violet; or yellow, yellow-orange, and orange. As a rule, the smaller the bed, the narrower the segment of the color wheel. Complementary (opposite) colors of the basic scheme should be used very sparingly to highlight the planting. For example, if you decide on a blue-violet, violet, and red-violet garden, a touch of yellow would be useful. A red-orange, red, and red-violet scheme could be high-lighted by the opposite color, green, in the form of foliage. This highlighting can be a tricky business, however, so in order to be safe, stick to white as an accent until you get the feel of using colors in landscaping. Occasionally, single complementary colors can be used effectively. For example, a golden yellow dwarf marigold blends well with the bright blue of lobelia. Foliage often provides enough of a color contrast. One way to test out your color scheme is to go to a dry goods store and place various colors of silk flowers next to each other. You will be able to see if the colors clash.

• When planning a distant planting keep in mind that the hot colors—red, yellow, and orange—will make the planting seem closer to the eye, while the cool colors—blue, purple, and green—will recede and appear to be more distant.

• When you install a bed or border, plant in groups of at least five or seven. (For some reason, even numbers of plants tend to appear as blocks of foliage and color in the garden.)

Calendula and centaurea

this book, they too are important plants in any landscape. (Ferns are also perennial, although they do not bear flowers.)

To maintain their vigor, most herbaceous plants must be divided regularly and replanted, and any mature perennial planting produces many more specimens than a gardener can use. One of the most satisfying ways to expand your garden is by taking extra perennial stock from friends, family, and neighbors. Don't be shy about asking, for every garden begins this way. One word of warning! Be sure to have the donor identify his or her offerings. Avoid just sticking any old plant you have been given in the ground willy-nilly without knowing exactly what it is. If you do, the result will most likely turn out to be an unruly hodgepodge of heights, textures, and blossom, often in clashing colors. If someone does give you unidentified stock, you can always plant it temporarily in what gardeners call a holding garden. This is a place where you can watch a plant grow to maturity for a season or two and decide exactly where it will or will not work in your garden.

Digging plants from the wild for your garden is not a good idea. Not only is it bad for the environment but in many cases it is illegal and subject to heavy fines. It is much better to identify the plant you like and purchase new stock or seeds from a native plant nursery.

Some mail-order supply houses offer perennial garden packages already planned for color combinations, gradation of height, and growing conditions. These can be a good investment for the beginning gardener.

## Planting and Maintaining Hardy Plants

You can buy hardy plants (trees, shrubs, grasses, herbs, and perennials) either at a nursery or garden center, or from a mail-order company. Whatever you do, I recommend that you browse through mail-order catalogues before buying. Will trees and shrubs be healthier or "fresher" if you buy them at a nursery? Not necessarily. Very few nurseries and garden centers grow their own stock; most purchase it from wholesale dealers, and even though you may buy the stock locally, it does not mean that it was grown locally. A tree or shrub purchased "on the ground," so to speak, may not be better, but it is likely to be bigger than anything that comes in the mail, which may be decisive for you if you're in a hurry to see your garden as you envision it. Just don't expect the breadth of selection locally that you see in catalogues. Finally, if there's a local gardening service that has a good reputation, you might use it for purchasing and planting trees. A good service will take responsibility for the long-term health of the tree and replace it if something goes wrong.

Trees and shrubs are usually sold in containers or bagged and burlapped (called "B&B" in the garden business). The burlap is very loosely woven and will even-tually rot, so it is not necessary to remove it before installing a plant. For environments that are particularly harsh, container-grown plants stand a better chance of surviving than B&B stock. Avoid bare root stock and be careful of B&B stock late in the season, for if the nursery hasn't been conscientious about watering, what you take home may resemble a cannonball with a stick in it rather than a tree. Perennial plants other than shrubs and trees are almost always sold in containers.

Although spring is usually the time when gardeners install new plantings of shrubs, hedges, trees, and perennial plants, recent research has shown that early fall is also a good time. A plant's roots continue to grow until the very cold days of January or February—long after the rest has gone dormant—and a strong root system is what a plant needs to endure the dry heat of summer.

The rule of thumb for planting is to make the hole twice as wide and twice as deep as the root ball. Assuming that you haven't improved the soil on your entire property, now is the time to mix about two-thirds organic material (topsoil, compost, peat moss, or well-rotted manure) with one-third of the excavated soil. Even if your soil is already excellent, friable loam, it is still a good idea to enrich the area where you intend to plant with organic matter. Fill the hole with the enriched soil and water it thoroughly. If possible, let it settle for a day before planting in it.

Planting is a cinch. Remove the soil you prepared the day before, position the plant in the hole at the level at which it was grown at the nursery, and fill in beneath, around, and on top of the roots or root ball, tamping the soil and watering as you work to ensure that you are not leaving any air spaces around the roots. When you are done, water the plant thoroughly and tamp the soil firmly once more. Be sure to leave a slight depression in the soil around the plant to facilitate watering throughout the season.

Give your plants growing space. Don't cramp shrubs and trees. Remember that although your planting may look very sparse now, the plants will grow to their mature size in several years, and you don't want them to crowd each other out. It is hard to resist the temptation of installing plants too close together, and even the most experienced gardeners do it over and over again. In perennial plantings, a good rule of thumb is that tall-growing plants should be planted two feet apart, medium-height plants eighteen inches apart, low-growing plants twelve inches apart, with tiny, miniature plants perhaps six inches apart.

Most plants need very little care beyond general watering and feeding. The one chore you should get in the habit of doing is to deadhead your perennials, that is, remove the spent blossoms. Not only does this make the plants look better but in some cultivars it helps to produce a second bloom. You don't deadhead flowering trees and shrubs (thank goodness), but you should remove old flower heads from lilacs, deciduous azaleas, and rhododendrons to improve next season's bloom. Unruly shrubs and vines can be pruned in the spring, with the exception of certain plants that bloom only from old wood and should be pruned right after flowering (see the plant lists for further information). Experience and the specific horticultural instructions that come with each plant are good teachers in this regard. Always prune damaged trunks and branches in the aftermath of a storm.

Remember, no plant is immortal. When a perennial becomes overgrown or seems to have lost its vigor, dig up the plant in the spring, divide it, that is, break the crown gently into several pieces, each with its own roots, and plant what you want to keep. Give the rest to an aspiring gardener or friend.

Once a planting is installed, another essential chore is to mulch. This holds true for all plants in your garden. Mulch perennials, vegetables, ferns, grasses, herbs, bulbs, and annuals. Cover the soil around all plants with at least two to three inches of organic mulch. This serves to conserve moisture, to keep weeds down, and, eventually, if you use an organic mulch, to enrich the soil. Mulch is worth its weight in gold, and it will save you hundreds of precious hours of work as well as many disappointments.

There are many different kinds of material that you can use for mulch, and your choice will depend in part on what is available and what you think looks good. The best is homemade compost (which is simply decomposed plant residues, usually mixed with manure). With a little bit of effort and planning, you can have large supplies of what gardeners call "brown gold" at a very good price: for nothing. Even if you don't purchase or build a composter, you can simply make a compost pile in an inconspicuous corner of your garden by alternating six-inch layers of organic plant material, including wet vegetable garbage from the kitchen such as coffee grounds and vegetable parings, along with leaves, grass clippings, and weeds, mixed with some soil and two-inch layers of manure. The pile should be roughly flat or concave on top to conserve as much moisture as possible. Experience shows that you need about a cubic yard of material to generate compost. After a season or so, you will have plenty of compost to enrich the soil and to use as mulch.

Oak leaves and pine needles provide an airy cover for the ground and improve the soil. Some other leaves, such as maple, tend to mat on the surface of the soil and can be harmful to plants unless they are reduced to compost. Grass clippings and peat moss are not recommended. A two-inch layer of pebbles can be quite attractive around trees, hedges, or shrubs that are growing within the brickwork of a patio. They will help to conserve moisture and to keep the weeds down, although they do not add nutrients to the soil.

If you opt to purchase mulch from a nursery, garden center, or landscaping service, it's probably best to use salt hay or wood chips, usually cedar or pine, in the smallest size you can find. Although the large chips may look reasonably attractive, they do not decompose readily enough. If you use wood chips, you should be aware that they will monopolize the nitrogen available to your plants while they decompose and fertilize accordingly. Buckwheat hulls are too light to use in country environments, most of which are windy, as are cocoa shells, which can be somewhat distracting in a garden on account of their chocolate scent.

Fall plantings should be protected by a six-inch layer of mulch over the winter. While hardy plants will not be harmed by the cold, constant freezing and thawing of the surrounding soil can cause them to heave up out of the ground. The salt hay keeps the soil at a more constant temperature, making it less likely that a plant will heave.

Well-mulched soil retains moisture well, but during prolonged periods of summer drought you will still need to water to a depth of a foot to a foot and a half at least once a week. You can check this by digging a place in the garden where plants do not grow but which has been watered. Lay down drip hoses, available at garden and home improvement centers, in your garden and leave them there for the growing season. These are preferable to conventional sprinklers, which lose water to evaporation and runoff. If local ordinances prohibit watering, you really need to plan your garden using only the most drought-tolerant species.

Finally, you should fertilize your plantings. For best results, work about one tablespoon per square foot of all-purpose 5-10-5 fertilizer into the soil around each plant each spring before growth commences. If your soil is decidedly sandy, you should fertilize more frequently because inorganic nutrients leach out of sandy soil very rapidly. Be careful not to overfertilize plants. More often than not, fertilizer runs off into the groundwater, where it does more harm than good.

## Growing Annuals

I am a great believer in using annuals in the garden. As opposed to perennials, annuals are plants that live for a season, growing from seed in the spring, bearing flowers that go to seed, and dying with the first frosts, completing their life cycle in this short span of time. Almost all annuals bloom throughout the summer and early fall, and some continue past the first frost. A handful start blooming in late spring, particularly if they are given a head start.

Annuals are indispensable to the country gardener. If you are starting out, you can use annuals to learn to develop color schemes without the elaborate scheduling that a perennial border requires. Because they mature quickly, even the summer renter can create a paradise using annuals. And because they come in an astonishing variety of colors and shapes, experienced gardeners use them to introduce exotic or surprising effects in tandem with perennials.

There are two ways you can have annuals for your country garden. It's easy to purchase flats of seedlings at garden centers and nurseries. You can even buy full-grown plants for an instant garden. The disadvantage of this approach to growing annuals is that the industry still offers little more than about a dozen cultivars in a few varieties of each as seedlings, and these are the most common annuals grown. When you restrict yourself to these offerings alone, you have merely scratched the surface of the many charming plants available to you.

Better to grow them yourself. Whether you purchase your seeds from supermarkets, garden centers, nurseries, or mail-order houses, you can choose from many more varieties. Some can be planted directly in the ground after the last hard frost; others should be started indoors four to eight weeks earlier for a full summer of bloom.

Fortunately, it's a simple matter to avail yourself of varieties that do need a head start indoors. With a small investment of time and money, you can make a fluorescent light structure to start seeds. (A small manufactured unit will cost you about four times as much, but even at that it will save you money in the long run.) Purchase a four-foot-long industrial fluorescent light fixture. They cost between $10 and $20 in most home improvement centers. These fixtures usually come with two cool tubes. Substitute one warm tube for one of the cool tubes. There is no need to buy expensive, plant-growing fluorescent tubes. Either hang the fixture in a heated basement over a table or workbench or attach it to the bottom of a shelf in the house. You are ready to start seeds indoors at the proper time.

As the fixture should remain on for about fourteen hours a day, you may want to buy a timer if you don't wish to be bothered with the daily task of turning it on and off. You can start with one fixture, but you will soon find that you need at least two. Eventually, you will want three or four to accommodate all the plants you wish to start from seed.

You can sow seeds in just about any container imaginable: milk cartons, plastic containers, flower pots, aluminum trays, in short, anything that will hold a seed-starting soil mixture. Drainage must be provided, so if you use homemade containers, poke holes through the bottoms so that excess water can escape. There are also many products available in garden centers and nurseries that are made specifically for starting seeds. I use and swear by APS (Accelerated Propagation System) seed-starting kits,

Marigold field, Cutchogue, Long Island

available from Gardener's Supply Company in Burlington, Vermont (similar products are available from other companies). These are made of Styrofoam and include a reservoir arrangement that maintains even moisture for the seed trays for about a week between watering, which is especially helpful if you are starting seeds at a weekend house. A four-foot industrial fluorescent light fixture will accommodate three of these self-watering seed-starter trays.

You also will need the proper soil to start plants indoors. Do not purchase potting soil, as it is too heavy in texture to start seeds. Use a seed-starting medium, such as Terralite or Reddi-Mix, and moisten it lightly but thoroughly before planting the seeds according to the instructions on the packet, that is, either lightly covered with soil or on the soil surface. Start several seeds in each individual compartment if you are using seed trays. Label the containers carefully and place them under the lights with the soil surface about two inches from the light tubes. Raise the lights as the plants get bigger. If you are using

homemade containers, mist with room temperature water, using a mister available in garden centers and nurseries, to keep the soil evenly moist.

When seedlings are about one-half inch high, cut off all but the strongest in each compartment. Feed once a week with all-purpose liquid houseplant fertilizer at one-quarter the strength recommended by the manufacturer. Most annuals can be safely planted outdoors "after all danger of frost": a good rule of thumb is to follow the recommended time for planting tomatoes outdoors in your area. About one week before planting them outdoors, you must "harden off" your annuals to acclimate them to strong sunlight and cool nights.

For the first couple of days, place the containers outdoors in a shady spot during the day and bring them inside at night. The third day, put them in the sun for about half a day and in the shade for the other half. Finally, leave them in the sun for the entire day and bring them indoors only if the night is to be chilly. In any event, if it rains bring them indoors. If the plants start to look bleached, they are receiving too much sun and are not yet accustomed to the strong light. Move them back into the shade. After about one week, you can safely plant them in your garden where you want them. (If you are only at the house for weekends, you can usually accelerate the process without damaging the plants.) By the way, you can start certain perennials from seed following the same procedures.

Taking care of annuals is a cinch. Most prefer full sun and are not fussy about soil. Plant and mulch as you would perennials, keeping in mind that annuals that are quite small at planting time can become rather large very quickly. Annual plantings are, to a great extent, maintenance free. The one thing you must do is to deadhead spent blooms, that is cut faded flowers before they go to seed. The reason you do this is not just aesthetic but to extend their period of bloom. Once seeds have formed, the plant has accomplished its purpose: to regenerate itself, and it will stop flowering. By deadheading you frustrate this process and keep the plant blooming until frost.

Chrysanthemum field, Long Island

### Tips for Using Bulbs in the Garden

If you are going to invest your time and money in a large-scale bulb planting, you will want it to be in harmony with your landscape and to add beauty to your home and surroundings. Although rules are made to be broken, in general here are a few design basics you can apply to spring and summer bulbs.

• When planting the major spring-blooming bulbs (tulips, standard daffodils, hyacinths, and Dutch crocuses) always set them out in groups of at least twelve or their impact will be greatly diminished. It is best to plant twenty-four if your budget permits. "Minor" bulbs should be planted in groups of no less than fifty, preferably a hundred, or they too will be lost. Always plant at least six of the same variety of lilies; three of the same variety of dahlias, begonias, and caladiums; and twelve of most of the other summer-blooming bulbs, such as gladiolus, acidanthera, tigridia, and forth. This is the bare minimum.

• Never buy a rainbow mixture of bulbs. The result at bloom time will be a hodgepodge of color, ineffective and often messy looking.

• Avoid planting bulbs in a straight line or in a single circle around a tree or bush. The result will be unnatural-looking and somewhat ridiculous.

• When planting a bulb scheme, concentrate on two or three colors in each location but do not mix them together. For example, a cluster or drift of violet-colored tulips next to a drift of yellow and another of white looks more harmonious than clusters that include different colors.

• Decide whether you want a formal- or informal-looking bulb garden and then stick to your decision. Keep in mind that an informal garden is asymmetric and is thus more appropriate for the majority of country houses. Formal plantings are symmetrical and are appropriate for stately residences.

• Hyacinths and certain tulips—Darwin, lily-flowering, cottage, triumph, and Darwin hybrid—are somewhat tailored in appearance so use them sparingly unless you

# Bulbs

Among the greatest pleasures of spring for the gardener are hardy, spring-blooming bulbs, both the "major" varieties—daffodils, tulips, hyacinths, and crocuses—and the often overlooked "minor" varieties—scilla, grape hyacinth, snowdrop, and the charming glory-of-the-snow—as well as irises, lily of the valley, and allium. Just imagine driving out to your country house in April or May and being welcomed by thousands of daffodils, tulips, and other bulbs. Of course, if you do not live in or visit your country home during the spring, you may decide not to install any spring-blooming bulbs. That is a decision you will have to make yourself. But there are also summer-blooming bulbs—lilies, acidanthera, gladiolas, dahlias, and others—that you can plant for a nice touch of class and contrast in a summer garden.

You can plant colorful beds and borders using only masses of bulbs, include bulbs in mixed beds with perennials and annuals, or scatter them on the ground and then just plant them where they have landed for a natural effect. Many bulbs are suitable for naturalizing; they multiply and spread from year to year without human intervention. Other places to use bulbs are interplanted among foundation plants; along driveways; along walks; in rock gardens; amid ground covers; at the foot of walls; in front of evergreen hedges; along fences; around mailboxes; around birdbaths, sundials, or other garden ornaments; in distant stretches of your property; and in a charming dooryard garden directly next to the entranceway to your house where in the early spring you can enjoy the jubilant bloom of many of the smaller "minor" bulbs close up.

Planting requirements for bulbs are modest. Most want either full sun or partial shade in order to perform well. The exceptions are allium, which prefers only full sun, and lily of the valley, which prefers partial shade.

Very few thrive in deep shade, so avoid areas under ever-green trees, foundation plantings with northern exposure, and other areas of little sunlight. Bulbs will rot in water-logged soil and require good drainage to grow properly, so if there is an area on your property that is swampy or often flooded during severe storms, avoid planting bulbs there. All bulbs are virtually insect and disease free, and a bit of soil preparation at fall planting time and some annual feeding is about all the maintenance that they require. And every year beginning in late winter, they reward you with dazzling and glorious displays.

All spring-blooming bulbs must be planted in the fall. Minor bulbs should be in the ground by the end of September, daffodils by the end of October, and tulips can be planted as long as the ground is workable. Summer-blooming bulbs, most of which are tender and must be dug in the fall and stored over the winter indoors, should be planted in the spring after all danger of frost, with the exception of lilies, which are hardy and can be planted in either spring or fall. By the end of summer, spring bulbs start to appear on the shelves of nurseries, garden centers, and even supermarkets. There are also mail-order nurseries that offer huge selections. It is a good idea to write for catalogues by June and to place your orders by the end of July or early August. Most mail-order nurseries deliver bulbs at the proper planting time for your area.

When you go to the garden to plant bulbs, be sure to bring a ruler with you so that you can gauge planting depth and spacing properly. As a rule, plant bulbs about three times as deep as their diameter. You also will need fertilizer. For many years it was universally thought that bone meal was an essential fertilizer for bulbs. Experience and research have now proven that although it will not hurt the bulbs, neither does it help them. It is now generally acknowledged among horticulturists that all-purpose 5-10-5 fertilizer provides whatever nutrients bulbs need.

Tulips

want a very formal look. Species tulips, daffodils, and the "minor" bulbs are often better suited to an informal country planting.

● Lilies, dahlias, and other summer-blooming bulbs look best when interplanted with perennials, annuals, or shrubs. The stems and foliage of many summer-blooming bulbs, particularly lilies, are rigid and become unsightly after bloom. It is a good idea to overplant medium-high annuals on the lily bed or to interplant daylilies. The foliage of the daylilies and their long blooming period will hide the lily foliage and add color to the area once the lilies have finished blooming.

● Since bulbs begin bloom-ing in late February and continue on throughout the spring, arrange your outdoor plantings of early-blooming bulbs so that you can enjoy them from inside as well as outside. Chances are that with late winter and early spring cold and rain, you won't be spending too much time outdoors soaking up the floral display.

● For displays in distant parts of your property, plant large groups of a single vari-ety of bulbs in drifts rather than in symmetrical beds. The effect is more natural looking and eye-catching.

Dig a hole twice as deep as the recommended depth for the bulbs you are planting and mix fertilizer with soil at the rate of one tablespoon per square foot, three-quarters of a cup per ten square feet, or four cups per fifty square feet. Replace the soil to the recommended planting level and flatten out the bottom of the planting hole by patting it gently with your hand to provide an even surface for the bulbs so they won't fall on their sides in the hole when you fill it in with soil. Set the bulbs in place with the pointed ends up and press them gently into the soil. Cover them, tamp the soil down lightly, and water thoroughly. If there are dry spells in your area during the fall, be sure to water the planting at least once a week. Spring bulbs can be given a dusting of 5-10-5 fertilizer at the rate of one tablespoon per square foot when they begin to emerge from the ground. Plantings of summer bulbs will benefit from a six-inch mulch to conserve moisture, to keep weeds down, and ultimately to fortify the soil. Burrowing rodents love to eat many varieties of bulbs. See the section on pests, p. 124, for some very helpful information.

After bulbs bloom, you can remove spent blossoms but not the leaves, which supply the bulb with nutrients for next year's bloom. Allow foliage to wither and dry naturally, then you can remove it by either cutting it or gently pulling it from the bulb beneath. If you find the withering leaves unsightly, tie them up in bundles with string or rubber bands or hide them by interplanting the area with perennials or overplanting with annuals.

When buying bulbs, be sure you buy healthy ones. If ordering from a mail-order source, order only from reputable firms, some of which appear in the sources section, on page 179. (This does not mean that sources not listed are not reputable, just that those that are listed can be trusted.) If you are buying bulbs at a garden center or nursery, use your eyes. Look to see if the bulbs are healthy looking, free of mildew or diseases, unbruised, and without blemishes.

Then feel them. If they are firm and not soft or mushy, have no soft spots, and are heavy in relation to their size, they should be healthy. Although not of an aesthetic nature, this tip will prove invaluable: *Beware of bargains!* Bulbs are quite inexpensive in the first place, and bargain collections sometimes include bulbs of inferior quality. As a rule, you get what you pay for. There are, however, two exceptions. Many mail-order bulb suppliers offer mixtures of daffodils for naturalizing at reduced prices. They are certainly worth the money if you plant to naturalize them in meadow, woods, or under deciduous trees. The other exception is end-of-season sales at nurseries and garden centers. Individual varieties of bulbs often are reduced in price toward the middle of November. Since there is still time to plant, you might wish to consider buying some of these to fill in your landscape after your initial planting.

## Growing Vegetables

Certainly, one of the most joyous and gratifying experiences of country living is growing your own vegetables for the table. And it doesn't take a lot of experience or knowledge to do it. What could be more delicious than a fresh green salad made from a collection of varieties of lettuce straight from the garden? Who can resist picking a luscious red, ripe tomato in the heat of summer and taking a big bite out of it while it's warm from the sun?

Some vegetables require cold temperatures in order for the seeds to germinate. These vegetables are generally quite hardy and will withstand late frosts and even a snowfall. Plant them as soon as the soil is workable in spring. In most parts of the country this is in the end of March or the beginning of April. Included in this group are peas, onions, shallots, garlic, leek, celery, celeriac, salsify, lettuce, radishes, spinach, most greens (including cress, mustard, and arugula), and members of the *Brassica*, or cabbage, family: bok choy, broccoli, brussels sprout, cabbage, cauliflower, Chinese cabbage, and kohlrabi. These same varieties, if planted in June, will not usually grow satisfactorily because the temperature is too high for germination and healthy growth. A good index as to when it is time to plant is the soil. If it is waterlogged and very cold, it is probably too early to plant the above varieties. If the soil is friable—if you take a handful and squeeze it a bit and it remains reasonably granular—it is usually a good time to plant.

Certain vegetables require slightly cold conditions but somewhat warmer than the above vegetables. These include Swiss chard, beets, and carrots. Although some recommend planting these at the same time as the varieties above, I have found that spring rains often rot the seeds, and germination is better if I wait a month or so— that is, to mid-April or early May—before planting.

You must wait to plant some vegetables until all danger of frost is over and the ground has warmed up considerably (mid-May in New York). These vegetables are tender; they will die if exposed to cold temperatures. Included in this group are all members of the bean family, such as string beans, lima beans, and kidney beans, tomatoes, eggplant, squash (both winter and summer varieties), melons, peppers, cucumbers, pumpkins, and corn.

Early spring vegetables such as lettuce, radishes, members of the cabbage family, spinach, cress, and arugula can all be planted in late August or early September for a fall crop. Members of the onion family will not mature in time for harvest, so they are inappropriate for late planting. You can plant garlic in the fall, for it will winter over and grace you with an early spring crop. Beets may be harvestable before killing frost if you plant now, but carrots will not be. Do not plant any members of the bean family (tomatoes, eggplants, or peppers) or any of the vine crops (melons, squash, pumpkins, or cucumbers) at this time of

Farm stands, Long Island

117

year for they require hot weather to mature to eating stage and will not survive early fall frosts.

Vegetables that are best grown from seed include all salad greens, such as lettuce, arugula, cress, and mustard, peas, all beans, all vine crops, such as winter and summer squash, pumpkins, melons, and cucumbers, and most members of the cabbage family. Here's a time saving tip: Many of these vegetable seeds are available in biodegradable strips, evenly spaced out, so that when you plant all you have to do is place the strip in the soil and the seeds will be spaced properly. Although these strips cost a little more than packages of seeds, they are worth the investment. All vegetables have to be thinned out once they reach an inch or so in height, and with the strips you won't have to do this chore. Some varieties of vegetables require an early start under lights and indoors and these are best purchased in six-packs (plastic trays containing six compartments with one plant in each) from garden centers or nurseries. These include tomatoes, peppers, and eggplant. Although members of the cabbage family do grow reasonably well from seed, it is often much easier to purchase six-packs of these varieties as well.

There are a few vegetables that you'll need experience to grow. Cauliflower is one because rubber bands must be placed around the forming heads to hold the leaves around them in order to blanch them, that is, to ensure that heads are white. Cauliflower is also quite prone to insect infestation. Celery also is tricky if you want the pale green or white blanched product. If you aren't fussy about that, celery is easy to grow. You may find that the carrots you grow in your garden are quite good. However, the carrots available in supermarkets, which are grown in California, are usually better and sweeter than those you grow at home. Most of my farmer neighbors prefer the California carrots to growing their own. Radishes are prone to worm infestation if planted too late,

though most other early-planted crops are not. To protect plants against worms, simply scatter some wood ashes onto the soil surface and with a cultivator scratch it into the soil before planting your seeds. Birds and corn borers love corn, so if local farmers grow and sell corn, it is perhaps less trouble and cheaper in the long run to buy theirs rather than to grow your own.

## Do-It-Yourself Water Gardens

Perhaps the most important revolution in gardening during the past decade or so has been the popularity of water gardens. The creation of heavy-duty rubber liners and preformed fiberglass ponds has made the water garden, once a province of the rich, available to almost everyone. Although through my many years of gardening my life has been graced with untold numbers of sweet delights— the taste of a warm tomato picked from the vine, the clove scent of old-fashioned pinks, the blooming of my rose garden—none of these has gratified me more than my water garden. Goldfish and koi glide under its surface, occasionally jumping up out of the water, frogs leap about on the lily pads, all manner of unusual birds fly in for a quick bath, water lilies nod their heads, and flamboyant irises sway gently on the banks.

The sound of water as it splashes over the rocks is both refreshing and soothing. Ken Ruzicka, one of the country's top water-garden designers who helped me install my pond, says, "Water is the *life* of a garden!" My pond is my refuge, offering calm and respite. It reconnects me with nature and leaves me recharged. It has become the center of my garden, the place where I entertain, where I work, where I read, where I can go whenever I need a fix of tranquility. I'm sure that down the line, it's going to add years to my life. That alone may well be reason enough to add a water garden to your landscape.

You don't have to have an existing pond or a stream on your property. Filtering systems and pump equipment make it easy to install and maintain a garden pond. Several years ago, with a little help from my friends and Ruzicka, I spent two weekends putting in a water garden. Could you do it alone? Yes, if it's a small pond (not more than one hundred square feet), the land is flat, and you're in great shape. (The digging takes its toll.) For anything complicated or large, another pair of hands or more is essential.

Basically, all you need for your water garden is a liner, either heavy-duty 45-millimeter-thick rubber sheeting or a preshaped fiberglass form, a submersible pump, tubing, and stones for edging plus plants and fish. A filter and a fountain head are optional. Have an electrician install a moisture-proof outdoor outlet with a ground-fault circuit interrupter to run the pump. As far

as the liner goes, rubber is cheaper, more versatile, and lasts for years; fiberglass can crack on impact or in cold temperatures. Furthermore, with fiberglass your pond is limited to the shapes and sizes commercially available. Need you ask? I went with rubber.

Before you start digging, do some site planning. Originally, I wanted a pond in the heart of my rose and lavender garden. After walking around the property, I decided to site it beside a rockery, where it would blend more naturally into the landscape.

Once you decide where to put your pond, consider its shape. What would look best on your grounds, a geometric or a free-form pool? Formal rectangular or circular ponds work well on level expanses of land with boxy, linear houses. Irregular ponds meld nicely with informal, less structured country landscapes.

Installing a pond is only half the story. To turn it into a place of true enchantment, you need the right

plants. Start with water lilies and delight in the way they open in the morning and close at evening. In most parts of the country hardy water lilies will survive the winter, and you have your choice of white, yellow, pink, even red blooms. I also like snowflakes (*Nymphoides*), exotic plants with clusters of small white or yellow flowers, but these are not winter hardy north of Zone 7. Lotus plants need a lot of topsoil to root in but reward you splendidly with the magnificent blossoms and heady fragrance. I even have a special event when the lotus blooms, inviting friends over for a glass of wine to enjoy the blossoms. Each aquatic plant must be put in its own pot, then placed in the water at the recommended depth. As for the banks of your pond, grace them with irises and other bog-loving plants. To plant them, create minibogs by digging one-foot-deep holes. Line these with a rubber liner to one inch below the soil surface. Fill the holes with soil, and set in your plants. The final touch are the fish. You can stock your pond with fantails, comets, and, if the pond is at least three feet deep, flamboyant Japanese koi. Here's the formula: one inch of fish per square foot of pond. In other words, a ten-by-ten pond can accommodate a hundred inches of fish (fifty fish two inches long, twenty fish five inches long, and so forth).

## Wildlife in the Garden

Perhaps the most appealing aspect of country living is enjoying wildlife. Living in tandem with nature is a profound experience. It puts life's ups and downs into perspective. How about blessed events in our garden! A Carolina wren built a nest in a flower pot in our barn, and her adorable little flock gathered at the window in anticipation of her arrival with food. Our one resident rabbit gave birth to six little ones in the rock garden. A lost cygnet, which resembled a short ostrich, wandered in one summer afternoon. Flocks of quail live here.

Bird feeders

Although many varieties of birds and butterflies will visit your country garden, there are things you can do to attract more of them. Feed the birds, find plants that they like, provide nesting places and birdhouses and you'll be surrounded by scores of them, all wearing dazzling plumage left over from some of Josephine Baker's old costumes. Learn to hand-feed them, for it is truly an enchanting experience. They are light as a feather. Soon you will become proprietary about them and refer to them as *my* birds. Everyone does. As a side benefit, many birds eat their weight in pesky bugs each week.

Because there are both birds you will want to attract to your property and so-called "junk birds," such as starlings, grackles, blackbirds, and English sparrows—unattractive birds that drive away the more rare and beautiful species such as cardinals, bluebirds, goldfinches, and orioles—you must be slightly cagey about the kind of feeders you install. Most junk birds eat from tray feeders. Hanging feeders, usually long Plexiglas tubes that you fill with various seeds, are equipped with holes and small perches for the birds to rest on while retrieving the seeds. When you purchase a tube feeder, inquire about the

perches. Were they designed to make it difficult for the larger "junk" birds to rest on them? Are they specifically designed for the smaller birds? Some tube feeders are made to contain a mix of various kinds of seeds that birds find appetizing, and others are specifically designed to contain thistle. Those for thistle have smaller holes than those for seed mixtures. I have several of both since thistle attracts goldfinches and pine siskins, very beautiful birds that I want in my garden. Through the years, I have found that rather than stocking my tube feeders with a mixture of seeds, I stick to sunflower. Junk birds do not seem to like sunflower as well as millet and other seeds in the mixtures. For thistle feeders, I use thistle.

I feed birds thistle year around. After twenty years of feeding, I now attract several dozen goldfinches to my feeders. In spring, when the flowering dogwoods and other trees are in bloom, I hang the feeders in the trees and move them as the spring bloom progresses from tree to tree. For example, the contrast of the pink blossoms of a dogwood or flowering crab with the brilliant yellow goldfinches flitting around is a breathtaking site indeed. One very important thing to consider. If you start to feed birds in the winter, you must continue, as they will become used to finding the food that you put out and may starve to death if it is suddenly cut off.

You also may want to provide suet feeders, which attract chickadees, woodpeckers, nuthatches, titmice, kinglets, flickers, evening grosbeaks, and many other species of birds. This past winter, I had three different kinds of woodpeckers at my suet feeder at the same time. These feeders, made of wire screen attached to wood, are quite inexpensive. You fill them with suet, which is available at the meat department of your supermarket or at your butcher. You can even put scraps of steaks or roasts into these feeders.

Trays of cracked corn, placed in a distant part of

Chickadees, in particular, are very tame, once they get used to you. They respond very quickly to hand feeding, and it is pure magic the first time one lands on your finger and grabs a morsel of sunflower from your hand. They are, you will find, as light as a feather. If you're taking a nap wear a wide brimmed straw hat and place sunflower seeds on the brim. The birds will soon discover them and land on your hat.

*Left:* Goldfinches feeding

your property, will attract game birds: pheasant, quail, grouse, along with blue jays, mourning doves, grackles, and red-winged blackbirds.

The list of foods you can put out for the birds is a long one. Peanut butter smeared on tree bark is a favorite; stale bread, bagels, cake, leftover pasta, dried fruits, oranges, and apples are also popular.

You also will want to provide nesting areas for the birds. Here are some things to keep in mind when you place the houses. First, hang them out of reach of predators such as cats and raccoons. Then be sure to secure them firmly to the object on which you hang them. There is nothing more upsetting to a mother bird (and quite probably to you as well) than to see a birdhouse full of young birds fall to the ground. Birdhouses must be cleaned out each spring before mating season begins because most birds will not build a nest in a birdhouse that contains an existing nest. Many birdhouses available at retail outlets are not made to facilitate this yearly cleaning process. Don't buy any birdhouse that can't be cleaned out.

Another thing you must be aware of when purchasing a birdhouse is the size of the hole in the house. If you wish to attract desirable birds—chickadees, nuthatches, and wrens—to your house, the hole must be small enough to eliminate entry by pesky English sparrows and starlings. Inquire at your point of purchase about this or read any printed matter that comes with the birdhouse to be sure the entry hole is the right size for the birds you wish to attract. I do have one birdhouse with a hole that is not the correct size for the small birds, and larger English sparrows live in it all summer long. Rather than fight it, I have attached a small Union Jack to the house, thus turning a rather ordinary birding experience into one with some humor. As my late mother always said, "Well, they have to have a place to live also."

Not all desirable birds are seed eaters. However, all require water and like to take baths. You will attract many varieties of birds that would not visit your feeders if you install birdbaths. The same attracting quality holds true for water gardens, of course.

Attracting hummingbirds to the garden goes beyond purchasing a hummingbird feeder, which I have never found to be effective. They love to frolic on a misty water spray. If you set your sprinkler up on a small platform, chances are the hummingbirds will stop by for some playtime. Hummingbirds tend to favor trumpet-shaped flowers such as marsh mallow, columbine, impatiens, cardinal flower, bee balm, penstemon, petunia, scarlet runner bean, and salvia, particularly the red varieties. I have a large planting of crocosmia 'Lucifer,' which hummingbirds love when it is in bloom. Every year I plant bright red petunias in a window box just outside of my office window. Imagine my delight watching the hummingbirds stop by for some nectar while I'm sitting at my desk, pretending to work.

You also will want to attract butterflies to your garden. There are a few plants that are particularly attractive to them. Start with a butterfly bush. This serves as the magnet to attract them. Also plant butterfly milkweed, cosmos, purple coneflower, fennel, lantana, parsley, moss pink, pineapple sage, French marigold, Mexican sunflower, *Verbena bonariensis*, and zinnia.

If you would like to learn more about attracting birds and butterflies to your garden, go to the library and ask for a book on the subject. You will probably find your interest will lead you to buying your own books so that you can identify the birds and butterflies that come to your garden. The late Roger Tory Peterson was the grand old man of the bird-book world, so consider any of his books. Most communities have an active chapter of the American Audubon Society that hosts birding tours and provides information.

For better or for worse, you will have four-legged visitors in your garden: rabbits, deer, squirrels, raccoons, skunks, chipmunks, and so forth. Remember that they all feast on your plantings, and although they are beautiful to watch, you are better off enjoying those that wander onto your property rather than trying to attract more.

## A Word About Pests and Lyme Disease

Many insects, reptiles, birds, and animals are the gardener's friends. Ladybugs, wasps, praying mantises, and fireflies consume not only the eggs of many harmful insects but in some cases kill the insects themselves. Birds offer colorful plumage and lovely songs, and some eat their weight in insects every week. Bats also are great insect eaters, consuming thousands of mosquitoes a day. You can attract them to your garden by installing bat houses, available from some mail-order garden supply houses. Bees pollinate flowers and make honey, and butterflies add much beauty to the garden. Toads, rapidly becoming endangered, consume ticks and many other harmful insects; snakes eat rodents, such as moles and voles. If you have an outdoor pet cat, it too will help to keep moles and voles under control.

Not everything in nature loves a garden, however. If your plants do not look healthy, inspect them carefully to determine what may be the problem. It is a good idea to bring a magnifying glass to the garden with you to expedite diagnosis. You can purchase remedies for the most common insect and fungal infestations. If you opt for chemical products, which are available at most nurseries and garden centers, always follow the manufacturer's instructions when using them to protect your health and the environment.

If you decide you do not want to use chemical sprays, use the so-called botanical sprays. Beyond that, many insects can be controlled with a spray made up of a half-and-half solution of dish-washing detergent and water. Don't expect a single application to rid your plants of pests. You will have to persist and spray every day for a week or so, and even then results are not guaranteed.

Rabbits and other small mammals are particularly hungry during the early days of spring, when plants that make up their normal diet may not have leafed out. They seek what they can just to survive. Now we all have some compassion for their hunger but not when they nip the emerging buds of our autumn dreams, that is, the bulb plantings that we worked so hard at planting last fall. Be thankful for small favors. They don't like daffodils, narcissus, crown imperial, snowdrop, *Iris reticulata, I. danfordiae*, lily of the valley, and scilla. They are ravenously addicted to crocuses and tulips. How many times have gardening friends told you that rabbits absolutely leveled every one of their emerging crocuses and/or tulips to the ground? I know gardeners who have totally given up on planting tulips and crocuses for this very reason.

Take heart, for there are humane solutions. Dried blood, available in garden centers, works for me. Beyond repelling our friends with the big ears, it is excellent fertilizer for bulb plantings. As soon as you see the tiny, green shoots of crocuses or tulips emerging from the ground, and this can be as early as late January, sprinkle some on the plantings. Don't worry about daffodils or the other bulbs listed above. The rabbits will ignore them.

Then, after each heavy rain, and you must be meticulous about this, repeat the application. I've done this for the past fifteen years or so and now have established plantings of crocuses and even tulips that have perennialized. I also have found that laying small pieces of chicken wire over a planting until the buds open works. Rabbits just don't seem to want to walk on wire mesh, and I can't say that I blame them. I remove the mesh when the crocuses

bloom and when the tulips reach about eight inches in height, carefully slipping it over the blossoms. If you notice that new growth on some of your perennials is being eaten, try the dried blood and chicken wire treatment until the foliage and emerging buds are about a foot high.

Unfortunately, dealing with moles and voles is not as easy. If you find yourself walking on grass that seems to sink beneath your feet or if there are long ridges of crumbled soil on the lawn, you probably have an infestation of moles on your property. Moles tunnel beneath the ground in search of insect grubs, which usually congregate around the roots of grass, plants, or bulbs. The moles eat the grubs but leave the plants alone. The only way you can get rid of the moles is to get rid of the grubs, which involves spreading all kinds of poisonous insecticides on the soil surface.

"Well, if the moles don't eat the bulbs, why should I worry?" you ask. Sometimes nature plays funny tricks. At work here is an insidious conspiracy, for after the moles make the holes in quest of the grubs, the voles, which resemble tailless little moles, go into the holes the moles make and tunnel through to the roots of plants and bulbs. Like the rabbits, they do leave daffodil and scilla bulbs alone, thank you very much, but most bulbs are three-star fare as far as they are concerned

Before I learned how to frustrate them, I had installed about one thousand bulbs, major and minor, in a rock garden here. The sandy soil in the garden, nicely warmed up by the rocks, was child's play to the moles and the voles. All of the bulbs bloomed the first spring, and then through the summer and fall the voles cleaned out the entire planting. The next spring all that came up were the snowdrops, daffodils, and scilla. A friend of mine, who had installed an extravagant bed of tulips, was strolling through his garden with friends and admiring the planting. Suddenly, right before their eyes, one of the tulips disappeared into a hole in the ground.

I had read somewhere that if you lined planting holes for tulips, crocus, and other favored bulbs with mesh gutter wire, it would frustrate these creatures. I tried it and it did help somewhat, but by the second year most of my bulb plantings were cleaned out. Then, several years ago, I was in northern Portugal, visiting the garden of vintner Antonio Guedes, and noticed the mole-made ridges in his lawn. I asked Guedes if he had mole and vole problems and he told me that he did but that he had come up with a solution. Wherever he wanted a planting of tulips, he excavated the area then sank heavy-duty plastic or rubber pots into the soil, with the rim of the top just below soil level. I tried it in my rock garden and it worked. I have several plantings of species tulips that are now in the eighth year, apparently vole proof.

Voles not only attack spring-blooming bulbs but also fruit trees, some perennials, shrubs, and ornamental trees. There isn't really much you can do about them except to get a cat. If a healthy plant suddenly seems to expire, chances are the voles are eating the roots.

Another rodent, albeit charmingly adorable, is the chipmunk. Like moles, voles, and rabbits, they savor crocuses and tulips. They also eat many varieties of annuals and perennials. An easy and humane solution is to purchase a Havahart trap for the chipmunks. Once they are caught, pick up the trap, drive several miles from your house, and release them. Although you may still have some chipmunk damage, the trapping and transporting help somewhat. Woodchucks are larger rodents that will eat many garden plants. They also can be trapped and carried off. It helps to have a dog to drive these rodents away.

Dogs also will help to keep deer off your property, although in areas with large herds deer always seem to win every argument. Deer, despite their great beauty, are anathema to all gardeners. All over the Northeast, mid-Atlantic, and Midwest areas, deer populations have risen dramatically in recent years, and few gardens escape their attention.

Although studies have been made to determine just what plants deer like or dislike, none are conclusive and all are riddled with practical contradictions. (The Cornell Cooperative Extension publishes a useful booklet, *Reducing Deer Damage to Home Garden Plantings*, which is available through their web site, www.cce.cornell.edu. There are some plants that appear to be reasonably deer proof, but, when their preferred food is in short supply and they are in danger of starvation, deer, like any living creature, will eat just about anything that grows in order to survive (just as the Dutch ate tulip bulbs during the German occupation of Holland).

Beyond installing tall fences, and they must be at least seven feet high to keep deer out, or electric fences, there are some steps you can take to protect your plants. All newly installed tress and shrubs should be wrapped with tree wrap or Tubex, available at garden centers and nurseries and from many mail-order companies. Deer are particularly hungry at the end of winter and in early spring, when there are few foliage plants around to sustain them. If you do have favorite plants that you wish to protect, provide some sort of cage fencing for them.

Deer repellents such as Ropel, Chew-Not, Deer Away, Bobex, and Hinder are available at garden centers and nurseries. Sometimes these work if you follow the package directions very carefully and start application before the damage is done. You need to repeat applications often, particularly after rain or snow may have washed the deterrents from the plants.

The intense debate about the widespread presence of deer in residential areas up and down the East Coast finally is not about nibbled plantings alone. It is about Lyme disease.

Although there are those gardeners who look upon Lyme disease as a gardener's status symbol, it is no laughing matter. The mere mention of ticks is enough to depress most gardeners. You must protect yourself against a tick-bite inflicted case of Lyme disease (first identified as an illness in Old Lyme, Connecticut, in 1975) and know how to treat it if you are gardening in the country. It is caused by a bacterium (a spirochete) and is transmitted primarily by the deer tick. If there are deer or field mice in your area, there will be ticks, for these animals carry the ticks from place to place on their bodies. Cases of the disease have been reported in almost every state, but it is most prevalent in eastern coastal areas from Maine to New Jersey, although it is spreading. Friends in Ohio say that it is rapidly approaching Cincinnati, and it is diagnosed with some frequency in Florida and California.

Lyme disease is sometimes difficult to diagnose. Deer ticks are very small–the nymph is about the size of a poppy seed–and people rarely notice them on their bodies until after they have been bitten. The most characteristic early sign of Lyme disease is the appearance of a rash (not necessarily at the site of the tick bite) that typically lasts two to three weeks. It may become as large as fifteen inches in diameter, but it will vary from person to person, and only about 50 to 75 percent of the people who get Lyme disease will develop the rash. Even if untreated, the rash will eventually fade. Other early symptoms of the disease are fever, headache, neck stiffness, muscle and joint pains, enlarged lymph glands, conjunctivitis, or general fatigue.

It is unwise to leave the disease untreated. The most common complication of untreated Lyme disease–coming weeks to months after the initial infection–is swelling and pain in the large joints, especially the knees. In 15 to 25 percent of untreated patients, neurological complications may eventually occur, and fewer than 7 percent of untreated patients develop irregular heartbeats or other cardiac problems.

If you are bitten by a tick or if you think you might have Lyme disease, you should consult a doctor, and preferably one who is familiar with the disease. Prompt treatment with antibiotics is usually effective. I was diagnosed positive this past summer. The doctor prescribed three weeks of antibiotics, and apparently I have been spared any serious discomfort or complications.

There is no way that an active gardener can completely protect himself or herself against tick bites in country areas that have deer and rodent populations. Deer ticks rest on vegetation wherever deer are found and are brushed onto humans or animals as they pass by. The spring, when the ticks are in the nymph stage and therefore most difficult to detect because of their small size, is precisely when most gardeners are busiest and not in the mood to take cumbersome precautions. However, certain measures should become habitual: You should wear light-colored clothing with long pants tucked into socks, long sleeves, and gloves when gardening in areas with underbrush; you should check yourself and your companion or children once a day for ticks (children ages five to nine are considered at high risk to get the disease); you should check your pets regularly for ticks; and you may want to use tick repellents containing the chemical deet on your clothing (following the instructions carefully). Deer ticks are found in heavily shaded, damp areas with abundant leaf litter and undergrowth. Fence deer out; mulch borders and shrubbery carefully; remove leaf litter from areas where you will be gardening or relaxing; and admire the brush-covered areas of your property from afar and try to keep kids and pets out of them.

There are pesticides that can be used to curb the tick population, but most of us are uncomfortable with the idea of exposing ourselves and our loved ones, not to mention our neighbors, to the possible long-term effects of pesticides. One habitat-targeted product is Damminix, which is disseminated in cotton balls that are supposed to be attractive to mice as nesting material and is the equivalent of dusting field mice with tick powder. According to the Cornell Cooperative Extension, the impact of Damminix on tick populations in New York State trials has been disappointing. If you use it, follow the instructions carefully.

A vaccine for Lyme disease called LIMErix was approved by the U.S. Food and Drug Administration at the end of 1998. The treatment, which is 80 percent effective and available to people between the ages of fifteen and seventy, requires three shots over the course of a year. It is probably wise to get the vaccine if you garden in the country, but you should continue to take the precautions described above.

Sunflower

Heliotrope

*Left:* Cleome and Japanese anemones

Plants in the following lists have been selected because they are hardy and easy to grow. Drought-resistant plants are marked with an ❀. Select these if your gardening time is limited. Plants that are attractive to birds are marked with a ➤. Note that almost all berry-bearing plants will attract birds. This can be a mixed blessing, because the birds eat the berries. Plants that are thought to be resistant to deer damage are marked with a 🦌. I say "thought to be" because very few plants are one hundred percent deer proof. In this department, it is best to collect as much local lore as you can.

# Annuals

All of the following annuals can be grown in all zones until a light or killing frost, depending on variety. Some annual seeds need light to germinate and should not be covered with soil–follow instructions on package.

### *Ageratum* 🦌
Clusters of soft, powder puff blossoms in various blue shades, as well as white and pink. Medium-green foliage. 12–24", depending on variety. Thrives in partial shade. Needs some moisture. Start indoors eight weeks before last frost date in your area. Deadhead throughout season for continuous bloom. Ageratum combines well with pale yellow-blooming and silver-foliage plants.

### *Antirrhinum* (Snapdragon) 🦌
Spikes of single, double, and butterfly-shaped blossoms in all colors except true blue. Medium-green foliage. 6–48", depending on variety. Thrives in full sun in enriched soil but will tolerate some shade. Needs some moisture. Start indoors eight weeks before last frost date in your area. Pinch tips of plants when about 3" tall to encourage branching. Then pinch again when new shoots are 3" tall. For continuous bloom, deadhead spent flower stalks. Snapdragons often winter over in moderate climates. Usually, the second year's bloom is even more spectacular than the first. Because taller varieties must be staked, select from dwarf or medium height varieties.

### *Arctotis* (African daisy) ❀
Brilliant yellow, salmon, apricot, orange, or white daisylike flowers. Gray, woolly foliage. 12". Thrives in full sun and well-drained soil. Seedlings resist early spring cold. Sow seed in situ as early in spring as ground is workable. For continuous bloom, deadhead spent flower stalks.

### *Begonia* X *semperflorens-cultorum* (Wax begonia) 🦌
Pink, salmon, coral, red, white, and bicolor clusters of blossoms. Stiff, waxy deep-green or bronze-toned, rounded foliage. 3–12", depending on variety. Thrives in partial shade and enriched soil but tolerates full sun. Needs some moisture. Start indoors six weeks before last frost date in your area. It is not necessary to deadhead spent flowers for continuous bloom.

### *Brachycome iberidifolis* (Swan River daisy) ❀
Soft blue, daisylike flowers. 12". Thrives in full sun and sandy soil. Start indoors eight weeks before last frost date in your area. Deadhead for continuous bloom.

### *Calendula officinalis* (Pot marigold) ➤
Yellow, gold, orange, apricot, or cream single and double dai-

sylike blossoms. Medium-green foliage. 24". Thrives in full sun. Needs some moisture. Seedlings resist early spring cold. Sow seed in situ about four weeks before it is time to set out tomatoes in your area. For continuous bloom, deadhead throughout season. Flowers are edible and can be used as a garnish in salads.

**Calliopsis, see *Coreopsis***

**Callistephus chinensis (China aster)** 🌱
Red, pink, purple, blue, or white pomponlike blossoms. Dark-green foliage. 6–30", depending on variety. Thrives in full sun and enriched soil but partial shade extends life of individual blooms. Needs some moisture. Start indoors six weeks before last frost date in your area. For continuous bloom, deadhead spent flower stalks. This is one of the most popular of all annuals, especially for fall gardens. Avoid planting asters in the same place two years in a row as they will not thrive in the same spot the second year.

**Celosia cristata (Cockscomb)** 🐾
Brilliant red, orange, apricot, yellow, and fuchsia blossoms. Medium-green foliage. 9–24". Thrives in full sun and well-drained, enriched soil. Sow in situ after all danger of frost. Thin to about 12" apart. Deadhead regularly to encourage more bloom. Blossoms of varieties in the plumosa group are feathery. Many gardeners consider celosia garish, and the colors can be overwhelming in the garden.

**Centaurea (Cornflower, bachelor's button)** 🐾 🌱
Blue, pink, white, and maroon thistlelike flowers. Silver-green foliage. 24–30". Thrives in full sun. Seedlings resist early spring cold. Sow seed in situ about four weeks before it is time to set out tomatoes in your area. For continuous bloom, deadhead spent flower stalks. Cornflower is easy to grow, but if you fail to deadhead after bloom the plant will bloom itself to death and become unsightly by midsummer.

**Cineraria maritima, see *Senecio cineraria***

**Cleome (Spider flower)** 🐾 🦌
Large rose, pink, lilac, purple, or white spiderlike blossoms. Lobed foliage. 3–6'. Thrives in full sun and light, sandy loam. Seedlings resist early spring cold. Sow seed in situ about four weeks before it is time to set out tomatoes in your area. For continuous bloom, deadhead spent flower stalks. Although stems grow tall, they are quite sturdy and rarely need staking. Cleome self-seeds freely once established. Local lore where deer are plentiful holds that they will not eat cleome.

**Coleus**
Grown for colorful foliage in brilliant red, mahogany, green, yellow, white, blue, or rose. To 24". Thrives in partial shade in enriched soil. Needs some moisture. Sow outdoors after all danger of frost. Keep constantly moist until established. Exotic foliage adds a tropical touch to any garden.

**Consolida ambigua (Rocket larkspur, annual delphinium)**
Blue, red, pink, white, or purple spikes of florets. Medium-green foliage. 3–4'. Thrives in full sun and enriched soil. Needs some moisture. Seedlings resist early spring cold. Sow seed in situ as early in spring as ground is workable or in the fall, as seeds will winter over nicely but will not germinate in warm weather. For continuous bloom, deadhead spent flower stalks. Rocket larkspur is a good substitute for delphiniums, which can be difficult to grow. Self-seeds freely in most areas.

**Coreopsis basalis/Coreopsis tinctoria** 🐾
Yellow, orange, red, maroon, or crimson daisylike blossoms. Medium-green foliage. 8–48". Thrives in full sun in well-drained soil. Seedlings resist early spring cold. Sow seed in situ four weeks before it is time to set out tomatoes in your area. Sow where plants are to bloom as coreopsis resents being transplanted. Where winters are mild (Zones 7–9), sow seed in the fall. For continuous bloom, deadhead spent flower stalks.

**Cosmos** 🐾 🌱
Bright clear red, rose, pink, yellow, white, or crimson daisy-shaped blossoms. Feathery foliage. 3–6'. Thrives in full sun in

well-drained soil. Sow in situ outdoors after all danger of frost. To encourage branching and thus more flowers pinch tips of plants when they are 12" high and then again when 18" high. For continuous bloom, deadhead spent flower stalks. Cosmos self-seeds freely once established and attracts birds.

### *Datura metel* (Angel's trumpet) ✺ ☘

Scores of enormous 8"-long, large trumpet flowers in white, yellow, blue or rose, depending on variety, on handsome 7"-long medium-green foliage. You can literally sit and watch the blossoms of this sensational plant slowly open in the evenings, and the scent is lovely. Treat as annual through Zone 6. In Zone 7, it is hardy and self-seeds prodigiously. 'Alba' is white, 'Caerulea' is blue, and 'Ivory King' a creamy yellow.

### *Dianthus* (Pinks, carnations) ✺ ☘

Brilliant-colored scarlet, salmon, white, yellow, pink, or crimson carnation-shaped blossoms on attractive silver-green foliage. 6–36". Thrives in full sun in well-drained soil. Sow in situ after all danger of frost. For continuous bloom, deadhead spent flower stalks. Avoid taller variety that grows on spindly stems. Flowers possess an evocative clove fragrance known to drive gentle persons into frenzies of passion.

### *Dyssodia tenuiloba* (Dahlberg daisy) ✺

Bright yellow, daisylike flowers. 12". Thrives in full sun in sandy soil. Start indoors eight weeks before last frost date in your area according to package instructions. Plants take four months to bloom from seed. Deadhead for continuous bloom.

### *Eschscholzia californica* (California poppy) ✺ ☘

Yellow, orange, cream, pink, or soft rose silky blossoms. Smooth, gray-green foliage. 12". Thrives in full sun in sandy soil. Sow outdoors after all danger of frost. For continuous bloom, deadhead spent blossoms.

### *Gaillardia* (Blanket flower) ✺

Large red, daisylike blossoms with yellow-tipped petals. 12–24". Thrives in full sun in well-drained soil. Start indoors

under lights six weeks before last frost date in your area or sow in situ after all danger of frost. There are also perennial varieties.

### *Gypsophila elegans* (Baby's breath) ✺

Tiny clusters of white or pink blossoms. Medium-green, lance-shaped foliage. 12–24". Thrives in full sun. Sow outdoors after all danger of frost. G. *paniculata* is the perennial species. Excellent as a backdrop for an annual garden, although some staking will be necessary in windy environments.

### *Helianthus* (Sunflower) ✺ ☘

Yellow or white daisy-shaped blossoms. Medium-green foliage. Suitable shorter varieties grow 12–48". Thrives in full sun. Sow outdoors after all danger of frost. For continuous bloom, deadhead spent flower stalks. During the past few years, sunflowers have become very popular with gardeners. There are many shorter varieties that are much more suitable for the average country garden than the familiar towering version. With these, you won't have to be concerned about wind knocking the plants down. By the way, if you're surprised by a sunflower you didn't plant, it probably grew from a seed a bird dropped.

### *Helichrysum* (Strawflower) ✺

Daisy-shaped blossoms in a wide range of colors. Medium-green foliage. 12–24". Thrives in full sun. Start indoors six weeks before last frost date in your area. Deadheading is not necessary. Flower stalks can be dried and used in arrangements.

### *Heliotropium* (Heliotrope) ☘

Clusters of deep-purple florets. Compact, bushy, deep-green or bronze foliage. 8–12". Thrives in full sun and enriched soil. Needs some moisture. Start indoors six to eight weeks before last frost date in your area. For continuous bloom, deadhead spent flower stalks. This old-fashioned favorite is highly fragrant, scenting the garden, particularly in the evening. Strangely enough, it is rarely grown in American gardens.

**Impatiens**
Pink, white, coral, salmon, red, magenta, purple, or orange blossoms. Deep-green foliage. 12–24", depending on variety. Thrives in semishade or deep shade in enriched soil. Needs some moisture. Start indoors under lights six to eight weeks before last frost date in your area. It is not necessary to dead-head. The tried-and-true flowering plant for shady areas.

**Impatiens balsamina (Garden balsam)**
Pink, white, coral, red, peach, and lavender spikes of blossoms. Deep-green foliage. 24–36". Thrives in partial shade or deep shade in enriched soil. Needs some moisture. Start indoors six to eight weeks before last frost date in your area. It is not necessary to deadhead. A good companion for impatiens in shade areas. Self-seeds freely in many areas.

**Limonium (Statice) ❀ ⚥**
Apricot, rose, purple, deep blue, light blue, white, or yellow sprays of florets. Medium-green foliage. 24–30". Thrives in full sun. Start indoors eight weeks before last frost. It is not necessary to deadhead. Blossoms can be dried and used in flower arrangements.

**Lobelia erinus (Edging lobelia) ⚘**
Intense blue, purple, burgundy, or white clusters of blossoms, some with white eyes. Mounded, fragile, medium-green foliage. 8". Thrives in partial shade in sandy soil. Needs some moisture. Start indoors six to eight weeks before last frost date in your area. It is not necessary to deadhead. Cascading varieties, such as 'Blue Cascade,' are spectacular in hanging baskets. If mound-form 'Crystal Blue' is too intense for your scheme, use 'Cambridge Blue,' a paler shade.

**Lobularia maritima (Sweet alyssum) ❀ ⚘**
White, rose, or purple florets. Mounded medium-green foliage. 4–8". Thrives in full sun or partial shade in well-drained soil. Sow in situ after all danger of frost. Be patient as germination can be slow. A tough plant ideally suited to any environment. Self-seeds freely once established.

**Matthiola (Stock)**
Well-formed spikes of double florets in violet, lavender, rose, red, or white. Handsome medium-green foliage. 10–18". Thrives in full sun. Needs some moisture. Start indoors six to eight weeks before last frost date in your area. For continuous bloom, deadhead spent flower stalks. Stock is an old-fashioned, heavily fragrant plant that (like the similar wall-flower, cheiranthus) is rarely grown in American gardens. Select from dwarf varieties as taller types must be staked to protect them from wind damage.

**Moluccella laevis (Bells of Ireland) ❀**
Greenish-yellow spikes of bell-shaped florets. Medium-green foliage. 24–36". Thrives in full sun. Start indoors eight weeks before last frost. It is not necessary to deadhead. Unusual green blossoms add an exotic touch to the garden.

**Nicotiana (Tobacco plant)**
Predominantly white but also red, pink, yellow, and purple star-shaped blossoms. Coarse medium-green foliage. 24–48". Thrives in full sun. Needs some moisture. Start indoors six weeks before last frost date in your area. For continuous bloom, deadhead spent flower stalks. Very fragrant, with a tobacco scent. Some varieties bloom at night.

**Nigella (Love-in-a-mist) ❀ ⚥**
Spidery blue, purple, pink, or white blossoms. Medium-green foliage. To 24". Thrives in full sun in well-drained soil. Sow outdoors after all danger of frost. Self-sows in milder climates. A tough old bird, love-in-a-mist can be dried and used in flower arrangements.

**Pelargonium X domesticum (Zonal geranium) ⚘**
This is the standard garden geranium, used throughout the world to decorate patios. Bright red, pink, salmon, or white flowers. Coarse, hairy leaves with rings of color. To 24". Thrives in full sun. Water during long summer drought. Start indoors six weeks before last frost date in your area according to package instructions, root from cuttings

taken from houseplants, or purchase plants. *P. peltatum* (ivy-leafed geranium) is useful in hanging baskets and withstands wind.

## Petunia

Scores of colors and combination of colors of these trumpet-shaped blossoms are available. Fuzzy, low-growing, medium-green foliage. Thrives in full sun in enriched soil. Needs some moisture. Start indoors eight weeks before last frost date in your area. For continuous bloom, it is very important to deadhead spent flower blossoms and stalks. Suitable for container plantings or hanging baskets. For beds, I recommend the single-flowered F1 hybrids of the variety often called *Petunia multiflora* in catalogues. *P. integrifolia* is a miniature petunia with a creeping habit: this tender perennial (hardy to Zone 8) is best treated as an annual.

## Phlox ✿

Buff, pink, salmon, red, blue, purple, orange, or yellow clusters of blossoms. Attractive medium-green foliage. 7–12". Thrives in full sun. Sow seeds outdoors after all danger of frost. For continuous bloom, deadhead spent flower stalks. Easy to grow and available in a wider color range than perennial phlox.

## Portulaca ✿ ⌖

Single and double red, pink, yellow, orange, salmon, coral, or white blossoms. Succulent, sprawling foliage. 6". Thrives in full sun in sandy soil. Sow outdoors after all danger of frost. It is not necessary to deadhead. An ideal container plant as the succulent leaves store water.

## Salpiglossis sinuata (Painted tongue, velvet flower)

Red, purple, brown, yellow, and cream funnel-shaped, velvety blossoms, often veined with gold. Medium-green foliage. To 30". Thrives in full sun and enriched soil. Needs some moisture. Start indoors twelve weeks before last frost date in your area. For continuous bloom, deadhead spent flower stalks. An offbeat flower to use in arrangements. Often self-seeds in milder climates.

## Salvia (Sage)

Brilliant red and purple spikes of florets. Handsome, dark-green foliage. 12–48", depending on variety. Thrives in full sun. Needs some moisture. Sow outdoors after all danger of frost. When plants are 3–4" high, pinch tops to encourage branching and more flowers. For continuous bloom, deadhead spent flower stalks. Annual sage is considered garish by many. Purple *Salvia farinacea* 'Victoria' is much in favor, as it is always easier to integrate purples into a garden scheme than bright reds. Perennial sage is listed under herbs.

## Scabiosa (Pincushion flower) ⌖

Ball-shaped blue, white, rose, pink, salmon, crimson, or lavender blooms. Medium-green foliage. 3'. Thrives in full sun. Needs some moisture. Sow outdoors after all danger of frost. For continuous bloom, deadhead spent flower stalks. Easy to grow and rarely seen in American gardens.

## Senecio cineraria (Dusty miller) ✿ 🦌

Stunning silver foliage. 8–12". Compact, moundlike growth habit. Often sports inconspicuous yellow flowers that most gardeners remove. Thrives in full sun in well-drained soil. Start indoors six weeks before last frost date in your area. Cover seeds with soil or planting medium according to package directions. Plant seedlings outdoors after all danger of frost. Also called *Cineraria maritima*. Silver foliage can be used effectively to set off blue and pale yellow flowering plants. Stunning when planted in combination with heliotrope.

## Tagetes (Marigold) ⌖ 🦌

Gold, orange, yellow, white, or maroon single or double pompon blossoms. Deep-green foliage. 6–48", depending on variety. Thrives in full sun but will bloom in partial shade. Needs some moisture. Sow outdoors after all danger of frost. For continuous bloom, deadhead spent flower stalks. Tried and true, easy to grow, a perfect plant for the busy weekend gardener. If vivid oranges and golds are not to your liking, select from recently introduced white- and cream-colored varieties. Taller varieties may need staking in unprotected areas.

*Tithonia rotundifolia* (Mexican sunflower) ✿
Large scarlet-orange, yellow-centered dahlialike blossoms. Medium-green foliage. 30–36". Thrives in full sun. Sow outdoors after all danger of frost. For continuous bloom, deadhead spent flower stalks.

*Verbena* ❦
Red, pink, lilac, yellow, or white blossoms, often with white eyes, on large trusses. Medium-green foliage. Often fragrant. Verbena has a tendency to spread, with one plant covering a considerable amount of space by the end of the season. Thrives in full sun. Needs some moisture. Start indoors eight weeks before last frost date in your area. For continuous bloom, deadhead spent flower stalks.

*Zinnia* ⚘
Blooms come in all colors except blue and in sizes from miniatures to giants. Deep-green foliage. 8–48". Thrives in full sun. Needs some moisture. Sow outdoors after all danger of frost. For continuous bloom, deadhead spent flower stalks. When seedlings are 4" high, pinch tips to encourage branching and more flowers. Zinnias are prone to mildew, which can make them look unsightly. Some newer hybrids resist mildew.

# Berries

Although growing fruit trees is extremely complicated and time consuming, growing your own berries is a manageable project in terms of time and effort. And surely, part of the country living experience is being able to go out to the garden and pick your own fresh raspberries and other delectables from the world of berries for the table and for jams, preserves, and jellies. Here are varieties that you can grow almost anywhere in the United States. All are hardy to Zone 4, except blackberries, which are only hardy to Zone 7.

*Fragaria vesca* (Fraises du bois, Alpine strawberries)
Foliage is a tidy, medium-green with white blossoms that produce small pointed berries. 8–12". Thrives in full sun or partial shade. Water during summer drought. Plant 1' apart and divide every three years or so. If you can find them in the markets, which is almost impossible, fraises du bois can cost more than a dinner in a fine restaurant. They are easy to grow and reward you with small kernels of strawberries with such a wonderfully intense taste that, in no time flat, you will become addicted to them. Beyond their gourmet qualities, fraises du bois adapt well to traditional landscape patterns and are useful as a border edging plant.

*Ribes* (Currants) ⚘
Ribes is a large species that includes currants and gooseberries. With handsome foliage and shrublike form, currants are thornless and thrive in full sun or semishade. 3–5'. They prefer clay loam to heavy clay. They do not, however, like sandy soil. Water during summer drought. Plant 5' apart and prune annually by removing all three-year-old wood. Currants are rarely available in the markets. Black, red, and white currants are very sour berries, usually used to make jams that are eaten fresh or used to glaze pastries and hams, in pies, and in fruit syrups. Birds relish currants, so if you want any left for yourself, you will have to net your entire stand of bushes. Be sure to follow this advice. If you don't, you will not have one single berry left on your bushes. If you net, be sure that netting is secure so birds don't get trapped inside.

*Ribes* (Gooseberries) ⚘
The British, poor dears, who have never been known for their culinary skills, make jellies, jams, tarts, pies, and pastries out of gooseberries. They leave me totally cold. The berries are not particularly flavorful, the bush has thorns on it, and the growth habit is rangy. However, there are always diehards who will want to grow them anyway. Plant 4' apart in full sun or partial shade in clay loam to heavy clay. Prune old wood at the end of the season to keep plant vigorous. Water during summer drought.

Currants

Gooseberries

***Rubus*** (Blackberries, boysenberries, loganberries, dewberries) ☘

Mostly small shrubs, plant 3–5' apart in full sun. Be sure to water regularly during the season, particularly when berries are developing. They need plenty of moisture. At the end of each season, prune out all two-year-old canes. New canes will grow to replace them. Purchase only erect varieties rather than the trailing ones. Trailing blackberries have a very unruly growth habit, must be staked, and require a great deal of care. Erect varieties are a breeze to take care of. Blackberries are hardy only to Zone 7A. We've all sampled the wild blackberries so ubiquitous throughout roadside America, and, although they are sweet, they are nothing to write home about. The cultivated varieties are lusciously sweet, large in size, and make a dessert worthy of one's most treasured guests.

***Rubus idaeus*** (Raspberries) ☘

Small shrub, 3–5'. Plant 2–3' apart in a rich, friable soil, a prerequisite for growing red raspberries. If your soil is not up to par, fortify it with generous amounts of rotted manure compost and peat moss. Plant in full sun or partial shade and be sure to water regularly during the entire season. If asparagus is the king of vegetables, then surely raspberries are the queens of the berries. Utterly delicious, very expensive in the markets, and easy to grow, they are my first choice of a home-grown berry. I have always had raspberries in my garden. There are two kinds: everbearing, which bear berries both in the spring and the fall, and the spring-bearing varieties. Everbearing are smaller than the spring-bearing varieties, but you get two crops out of each plant every season. As with most berries, birds relish raspberries, so be sure to net your berry patch or you will have no berries left for yourself. Some gardeners construct small screen houses to enclose their berry patches. This is an easy project that anyone can do on a weekend. It is a very good idea.

***Vaccinium*** (Blueberries) ☘

I have never had luck with blueberries. No matter what I

have done, the birds always get to the fruit before I do. When in season, fresh blueberries are readily available; professionals do a fine job of growing them. You will save yourself time, trouble, disappointment, and frustration by picking them up in the markets when they are in season. For those craggy individuals who never take advice from anybody, blueberries like full sun, fortified acid soil, and sufficient moisture. Since they are handsome plants, you can use them in a shrub border if you are satisfied with their lovely pinkish white spring blossoms. If you want fruit, of course, you will have to net them. Good luck.

# Bulbs

## SPRING BULBS

Hardiness: All of these spring-blooming bulbs are hardy as far north as Zone 3, and should be planted in the fall. Since they are dormant in the summer, all bulbs are drought resistant.

### *Allium* (Ornamental onion)
True bulb, late spring/early summer. White, pink, purple, blue, or yellow round or flat flower heads and onionlike foliage. 4"–8'. Plant 4–8" deep, 3–8" apart, depending on variety.

### *Anemone blanda* (Greek anemone)
Rhizome, early/mid-spring. Bluish-purple, pink, red, or white daisylike blossoms. Medium-green, leafy foliage. 4–6". Plant 4–6" deep, 3–4" apart. Soak rhizomes in room temperature water for forty-eight hours before planting. The white variety is particularly effective when overplanted with 'Red Riding Hood' tulips.

### *Chionodoxa luciliae* (Glory-of-the-snow)
True bulb, early spring. Blue, pink, or white star-shaped blooms. Spearlike, medium-green foliage. 4–5". Plant 3" deep, 1–3" apart. Easy to grow. Chionodoxa multiply readily into substantial clumps.

### *Convallaria majalis* (Lily of the valley) 🦌
True bulb, late spring. Familiar, bell-shaped, white or pink blossoms. Broad, medium-green foliage. 8". Plant 3" deep, 3–4" apart. The foliage serves as an excellent, non-invasive ground cover in shady areas.

### *Crocus*
Corm, late winter/early spring. Gold, yellow, orange, lemon, light blue, lavender, purple, white, cream, or plum-colored goblet-shaped blossoms. Medium-green grasslike foliage. Plant 2" deep, 1" apart. Recommended varieties include *C. ancyrensis* ('Golden Bunch'), *C. angustifolius* (*C. susianus*), *C. chrysanthus* 'Advance,' *C. chrysanthus* 'Blue Bird,' *C. chrysanthus* 'Blue Pearl,' *C. chrysanthus* 'Canary Bird,' *C. chrysanthus* 'Cream Beauty,' *C. chrysanthus* 'Snow Bunting,' *C. chrysanthus* var. *fusco-tinctus*, *C. chrysanthus* 'Whitewell Purple,' 'Lady Killer,' 'Ruby Giant,' *Sieberi* 'Violet Queen,' and 'White Triumphator.'

### *Crocus vernus* (Dutch crocus)
Corm, late winter/early spring. Familiar deep-purple, white, yellow or lilac goblet-shaped blossoms. Medium-green grasslike foliage. 4–6". Plant 3" deep, 3–6" apart. Naturalizes when established.

### *Eranthis* (Winter aconite)
Tubers, late winter. Bright yellow, small, buttercuplike blossoms on 2–4" medium-green clusters of foliage. Plant 2" deep, 3–4" apart as soon as they are available in late summer. Soak in tepid water for twenty-four hours before planting. The most common cause of failure is late planting. Along with galanthus, it is the earliest of all the spring-blooming bulbs, often growing right through the snow. If conditions are right, it will naturalize.

### *Fritillaria* 'Goldilocks'
True bulb, mid-spring. Golden yellow clusters of blossoms. Erect, straplike foliage. 6". Plant 4" deep, 4" apart. A charming new mini-addition to the ever growing world of available fritillaria.

*Fritillaria imperialis* (Crown imperial) 🦌
True bulb, mid-spring. Red, orange, or yellow clusters of blossoms. Erect clusters of straplike foliage. 30–48". Plant 8" deep, 8" apart. The blossoms do not smell pleasant, so they are best kept away from dooryards or windows. All animals hate them.

*Fritillaria meleagris* (Guinea hen flower)
True bulb, mid-spring. Purple-and-white or white drooping, bell-shaped blossoms with checkered pattern. Grasslike foliage. 12". Plant 3–4" deep, 3–4" apart. Plants often naturalize once established.

*Fritillaria michailovskyi* (Michael's flower)
True bulb, mid-spring. Bronze-maroon, yellow-edged, bell-shaped blossoms. Straplike foliage. 8–12". Plant 3–4" deep, 3–4" apart.

*Fritillaria persica* (Persian bells)
True bulb, mid-spring. Deep purple-violet, very fragrant, bell-shaped blossoms. Straplike foliage. 36". Plant 8" deep, 6" apart. Particularly effective when set off by yellow and white daffodils.

*Galanthus* (Snowdrop)
True bulb. Translucent, white, bell-shaped blossoms. Slender medium-green foliage. Plant 2–3" deep, 2–3" apart. Along with *Eranthis*, it is the earliest blooming of all the spring bulbs. Once planted, leave them where they are since each year the bloom display will become more and more lush and dramatic.

*Hyacinthus orientalis* (Dutch hyacinth)
True bulb, early/mid-spring. Blue-purple, red, pink, yellow, cream, white, or orange flowerlets on columnar spikes. Jade-green straplike foliage. 8–12". Plant 5" apart, 6" deep. Familiar to all, hyacinths are easily grown in the garden. Their stiff appearance makes it difficult to use them effectively in most landscapes, but after the first year of bloom the stalks of flowerlets loosen up substantially, taking on a lovely, informal look. Their scent is unforgettable.

*Iris*, bearded, see Perennials

*Iris danfordiae*
True bulb, late winter/early spring. Yellow, iris-shaped blossoms. Grasslike foliage. 6". Plant 3–4" deep, 3–4" apart. Although they rarely boom a second year, these are worth the effort of planting every fall. Along with the *Iris reticulata*, they provide sparkling, late winter color in a country garden.

*Iris reticulata*
True bulb, late winter/early spring. Light blue, lavender, or purple iris-shaped blooms. Grasslike foliage. 6". Plant 3–4" deep, 3–4" apart. This low-growing iris often blooms as early as late February. Coupled with *Iris danfordiae's* bright yellow blossoms, they certainly lift the late winter doldrums.

*Leucojum*
True bulb, late spring. White, bell-shaped, pendant blooms. Straplike foliage. 12". Plant 8" deep, 6" apart. Particularly effective if planted in large drifts. They naturalize readily.

*Muscari* (Grape hyacinth)
True bulb, mid-spring. Bright blue, pale blue, or white clusters of blossoms. Sprawling, straplike foliage. 4–12". Plant 3" deep, 3" apart. Most flowers of these charming bulbs resemble bunches of grapes. They perfume the surrounding air with a lovely, subtle, sweet fragrance.

*Narcissus* (Daffodil) 🦌
True bulb, mid-spring. White, yellow, gold, orange, or apricot and combinations thereof depending on variety. There are eleven basic types of narcissus according to a system established by the Royal Horticultural Society of Great Britain and followed by bulb growers throughout the world. Shapes include the familiar trumpet, small-cupped, large-cupped, double, and so forth. All grow on erect 12–24" stems over swordlike medium-green foliage. Plant 8" deep, 6–8" apart, depending on size of bulb. Daffodils are probably the most universally grown and loved of all the spring-flowering

bulbs, for practical as well as aesthetic reasons: they are not only pest and disease free but rodent proof as well. Most varieties perform well for years. After about three years, some form thick clumps of foliage but steadily produce fewer flowers. If that happens, dig them after foliage withers, separate the bulbs, and replant. Proven varieties include 'Arctic Gold,' 'Binkie,' 'Campanile,' 'Carlton,' 'Cherie,' 'Dove Wings,' 'Duke of Windsor,' 'February Gold,' 'Flower Record,' 'Ice Follies,' 'March Sunshine,' 'Mrs. R. O. Backhouse,' 'Red Rascal,' 'Spell Binder,' 'Sweetness,' 'Sun Chariot,' 'Thalia,' and 'Trevithian.'

### Narcissus (Miniature daffodil)
True bulb, early/mid-spring. Yellow, orange or white and combinations thereof. Trumpet-shaped or double blossoms on 6–14" stalks, depending on variety, over medium-green, spearlike foliage. Plant 4–6" deep, 4–6" apart. These mini-sized versions of the standard daffodils add great charm to dooryard gardens, rockeries, and foundation plantings. Still, many gardeners have not yet discovered them. They are very reasonable in price and are a joy to behold in the spring.

### Puschkinia (Striped squill)
True bulb. Bluish white or white clusters of ½–1" blossoms on 4–8" stalks over straplike foliage. Plant 3" deep, 2–3" apart. Like chionodoxa, a fine companion plant, it will self-sow and naturalize if conditions are favorable. A bulb that should be more popular. This one is ideal for the spring garden, tucked here and there in the front of the border or by the dooryard.

### Scilla hispanica (Spanish bluebell)
True bulb, early spring. Blue, white, or pink spiked clusters of 1" bell-shaped blossoms on 12" stalks over medium-green, straplike foliage. Plant 3–4" deep, 6–8" apart. These semitall growing bulbs should be planted more widely. They are ideal for naturalizing in areas of partial shade or in woodland gardens. I prefer the blue or white varieties rather than the pink, which has a washed-out look when in bloom.

Hybrid Asiatic lilies

Crocosmia

Galanthus

Allium

Daffodils and muscari

Crocus

*Scilla sibirica/Scilla tubergeniana* (Squill)
True bulb, early spring. Brilliant blue, pale blue, lilac, pink, or white bell-shaped or star-shaped blossoms on 3–12" stems over straplike leaves. Plant 3" deep, 3–4" apart. With sensationally beautiful electric blue blossoms, *Scilla sibirica* is perhaps my favorite early-spring-blooming minor bulb. The blossoms of *S. tubergeniana* are pale blue or white and, although charming, do not make the visual impact of the *S. sibiricas*.

## *Tulipa* (Tulip)

In Holland, and indeed throughout Europe, most gardeners treat tulips as annuals, that is, they plant them in the fall and then, after bloom, dig them up and throw them away. They do this because they know that most tulips produce fewer and fewer blooms with each passing year. Here in America, however, we tend to think in terms of permanent, perennial plantings, so we plant tulips and then, several years down the line, wonder why they are no longer producing spectacular bloom. The reason is that tulip bulbs divide into small bulbs each year, and if the planting is not fertilized and the soil structure and climate are not ideal, they deplete. Even under optimal conditions, the blooms usually become smaller and smaller, eventually disappearing.

Therefore, in your garden, most tulips cannot be counted on after a year or two. Some varieties are more prone to "perennialize" than others—that is, to provide a continuing display year after year—but they must be fertilized properly to achieve this effect. Beyond this, conditions vary to such an extent from area to area, from garden to garden, and even within an individual garden that you cannot count on true perennialization of tulips.

There are many types of tulips available. Species tulips, most of which are the earliest to bloom and the closest genetically to the original wild tulips, include *T. kaufmanniana*, *T. fosterana* (the so-called emperor tulip), and *T. greigii*. All of these tend to perennialize and multiply, providing beautiful displays year in and year out. Early-blooming Triumph, later-blooming Cottage, Rembrandt, Parrot, Lily-flowered, and viridiflora tulips, and the hundreds of varieties of Darwin tulips, are not prone to perennialize, usually producing less and less bloom each year. The spectacular Darwin hybrids, a cross between *T. fosterana* and the Darwin tulip, do tend to perennialize if conditions are favorable. I have a planting of Darwin hybrid 'Gold Apeldoorn' now in its sixth year, more beautiful and with more blooms than when it was planted. In addition to the above, there is a class of wild or near-wild tulips that truly does perennialize. Small in stature and bloom, these tulips usually multiply freely and can be used in rock gardens, dooryard gardens, or anywhere they can be viewed closely. Most are early bloomers and are available from mail-order sources.

### *T. fosterana* (Emperor tulip)

Early/mid-spring. Red, pink, yellow, white, orange, and combinations thereof. Turban-shaped blossoms on 12–20" stems over medium-green or medium-green and purple broad-leafed foliage. 4". Plant 6" deep, 4–6" apart. These are tall tulips that tend to perennialize. Until recently, only solid colors were available, but each year, hybridizers offer new and interesting varieties, many multicolored.

### *T. kaufmanniana*

Early/mid-spring. Salmon, scarlet, yellow, cream, apricot, orange, and combinations thereof. Tulip-shaped and water-lily-shaped blossoms on 6–12" erect stems over medium-green, medium-green and burgundy, or medium-green and white foliage. Plant 6" deep, 3–6" apart. These are much lower growing than the Dutch hybrids and Darwins but are well-suited to country gardens.

### *T. greigii*

Early/mid-spring. Orange, red, yellow, gold, cream, pink, ivory, and combinations thereof. Tulip-shaped and water-lily-shaped blossoms on 6–20" erect stems over medium-green foliage usually mottled with purple or brown. Plant 6" deep, 3–6" apart. Generally larger than *T. kaufmanniana*.

**Tulip species**

Early/mid-spring. Yellow, white, red, rose, purple, or combinations thereof. Tulip-shaped blossoms on erect 3–18" stems over broad, medium-green foliage, some twisted. 1–2". Plant 3–4" deep, 3–4" apart. If these irresistible early-blooming miniature tulips are happy, they will multiply as they do in nature. They are certainly worth trying to see if they become established.

**Tulip, Dutch**

All colors except blue. Turban-shaped single or double blooms on 18–36", erect stems over medium-green, broad-leafed foliage, depending on variety. Plant 8–12" deep, 6" apart. There are a number of classifications of tulips beyond the species listed above. These bloom throughout the spring, and if you select from each category, you can have around two months of tulip bloom. In most country gardens, treat them as annuals, digging and discarding them after bloom. However, Darwin hybrids sometimes do perennialize. Install new plantings each fall. Just to sift things out for you, here are the various classifications according to bloom time: early spring: single early, double early; mid-spring: Mendel, Triumph, Darwin hybrid, double peony, viridiflora; late spring: Darwin, Lily-flowered, Cottage, Rembrandt, Parrot, double late.

SUMMER BULBS

Hardiness: Except for lilies, the following bulbs are tender and must be planted in the spring, after all danger of frost, rather than in the fall. They must be dug in the fall after foliage has withered or been killed by frost, dried, cleaned and then stored over the winter in dry peat moss or vermiculite in a cool, dry, dark place. They can be replanted in the spring. Treat lilies like hardy perennials.

*Acidanthera bicolor* (Abyssinian gladioli, peacock orchid)
Corm. Creamy white, mahogany-centered, 2", star-shaped blossoms on 18–24" spearlike, medium-green foliage. Plant in full sun or partial shade after all danger of frost, 3" deep, 4" apart. Scratch a light dusting of 5–10–5 fertilizer into the soil when leaves emerge and again three or four weeks later. Stake plants when 1' high. Water during summer drought. If you are north of Zone 6, it is easier to buy inexpensive, new corms than to winter them over. The blossoms exude a heavy, provocative perfume, more pronounced during the torpid heat of midsummer evenings.

*Canna* (Canna lily)
Rhizome. Red, orange, yellow, pink, cream, white, or bicolored, 4–5" blossoms on 18"–6' spikes over broad, bright green, blue-green, variegated green, and yellow or bronze leaves, depending on variety. Plant in full sun after all danger of frost, 1'2" deep, 15–18" apart. Scratch a light dusting of 5–10–5 fertilizer into soil every two weeks during the growing season. Water during summer drought. North of Zone 7, cut the stalks to the ground after they are blackened by frost, dig roots, and dry in an airy, shady, frost-free place for a few days. Store the rhizomes upside down in dry peat moss, perlite, or vermiculite, and replant in the spring. Be very careful in selecting the varieties that you wish to grow, as even a small planting will overwhelm almost any garden. The most wind resistant are the dwarf varieties (Pfitzer hybrids, 'Seven Dwarfs'), which are also more in scale for the average garden. Although the screaming reds, oranges, and yellows look inviting in garden catalogues and are even attractive in large public parks, the more subdued pinks, creams, and whites are far more suitable for a country home garden.

*Crocosmia* (Montbretia)
Corm. Yellow, orange, or scarlet 1½" blooms on 24–48" stalks with spearlike, medium-green foliage. Plant in full sun after all danger of frost, 3" deep, 4" apart. Scratch a light dusting of 5–10–5 fertilizer into soil when plants emerge and also three or four weeks later. Stake plants when one foot high. North of Zone 7, order and plant new corms each spring.

*Gladiolus*
Corm. Blossoms in every color of the rainbow on 1–5' stalks

with medium-green, spearlike foliage. Plant in full sun in sandy soil after all danger of frost, 6" deep, 5" apart. Scratch a light dusting of 5–10–5 fertilizer into soil when plants emerge and also 3–4 weeks later. Stake plants when 1' high. Water during summer drought. North of Zone 7, order and plant new corms each spring. Because they are very stiff in appearance, I have found that selecting the dwarf varieties and planting them in a clump, allowing them to flop over, softens gladiolus's harsh growth habit and adds just the right touch of informality to this flower usually associated with funerals.

## Lilium (Lily)

True bulb. All colors except blue. Depending on variety, 4–8" star- or trumpet-shaped blossoms on 2–7' stalks with glossy, dark-green leaves. Plant in full sun or partial shade in enriched soil. Set bulbs 6–8" deep, with small lily bulbs 6" apart and larger bulbs (those the size of a fist) 18" apart. Stake taller varieties as they grow but be careful not to drive stake too close to stalk as you might injure the bulb. Shorter varieties, such as hybrid Asiatic lilies, usually do not need staking. Lilies are among the few hardy summer flowering bulbs, and they do not have to be dug in the fall and stored indoors over the winter. You can use lilies in perennial borders and island beds, for masses of color among shrub borders, or incorporated within foundation plantings. A bonus is that lilies attract hummingbirds. These are the available cultivars:

Aurelian hybrids: These are the towering trumpet lilies that can grow to 8'. They look magnificent as a backdrop for a very wide border, but for most country plantings they are too tall.

Hybrid Asiatic: These are much more manageable and sensible for the country landscape than the Aurelian hybrids as they grow to between 2' and 4', depending on the variety. The flower spike is compact with many blooms, some in solid colors, others speckled. Be very careful when selecting colors as some can be quite startling, even garish.

L. lancifolium (Tiger lily): Most of these varieties are spotted, with the petals turned back. Each produces from twelve to twenty flowers per stem. They reach a height of 3–4'. Here again, be careful in your color selection as some varieties tend to be garish.

L. speciosum (Japanese lily): Many consider these the most beautiful of all the lilies. Colors are pink, rose, white, or gold and combinations thereof. Although they can grow to 5', they rarely need staking.

## Polianthes tuberosa (Tuberose)

Rhizome. White, 2" single or double blossoms on 15–24" stems, with medium-green straplike foliage. Plant in full sun in enriched soil in the spring, after all danger of frost, 3" deep, 6" apart. Scratch a light dusting of 5–10–5 fertilizer into soil one month after leaves emerge and every four weeks thereafter. North of Zone 7, order and plant new rhizomes each spring. Although foliage is rangy and blossoms are only mildly attractive, tuberose scent is so captivating that you might wish to consider growing them in your country garden.

## Tigridia pavonia (Tiger flower, Mexican shell flower)

True bulb. White, yellow, orange, scarlet, pink, lilac, buff, and combinations thereof. 5–6" blossoms on 18–30" stems with slightly untidy, spearlike foliage. Plant in full sun or partial shade after all danger of frost, 6" deep, 4–6" apart. Scratch a light dusting of 5–10–5 fertilizer into soil once a month during growing season. North of Zone 7, order and plant new bulbs each spring. Although each flower lasts only one day, the many buds on each stalk create a display for many weeks.

## Zantedeschia (Calla lily)

Rhizome. White, yellow, pink, lavender, bright red flowers on 1–4' stalks over large heart-shaped leaves. Plant in full sun in soil fortified with peat moss, 2" apart and 6" deep, after all danger of frost. Maintain even moisture until blooming ends. There are many new varieties available. For an early start, plant in pots indoors in March or April and set out after all danger of frost. The magnificent white calla variety is Zantedeschia aethiopica.

FALL BULBS

Hardiness: All are hardy to Zone 3. Since all autumn-blooming bulbs are dormant in the summer, they are drought resistant.

### Colchicum

Corm. Single and double varieties in deep lilac, lavender, pure white, and rose-pink, like a big crocus, on 4–8" stems over large glossy leaves. Plant in late summer or early fall for fall bloom. Set corms in full sun or semishade in soil fortified with peat moss, 3" deep, 4–6" apart. Maintain even moisture until blooming ends. Varieties include: 'Autumnale Album,' 'Cilicicum,' 'Double Waterlily,' 'Speciosum,' and 'The Giant.'

### Crocus, Autumn

Corm. Small, elegant, cup-shaped blooms 4–6" high in rose, pink, blue, violet, and yellow over grasslike foliage. Plant in August or September. Set out in full sun or partial shade, pointed end up, 3–4" deep and 2" apart, in light, well-drained, somewhat sandy soil. Many perennialize. They are a favorite of burrowing creatures such as voles, moles, and chipmunks. Varieties include: 'Cassiope,' C. sativus, 'Kotschyanus,' 'Kotschyanus Albus,' and 'Speciosus.'

### Sternbergia (Winter daffodil)

Corm. Bright yellow, crocuslike blossoms after long strap-shaped leaves die in the summer, and then flower until frost on plants 6–8" tall. Plant bulbs in early fall in full sun, 4–6" apart, 1" deep, in dry, well drained, heavy soil. They will perennialize and multiply but you must provide protection from burrowing moles, voles, and chipmunks.

# Ferns

All of the ferns listed below are deciduous except *Polypodium virginianum* (American wall fern), so you should remove spent foliage after a killing frost. All are hardy to Zone 5, and all require regular watering during the growing season.

### Adiantum pedatum (Maidenhair fern)

Native fern with lacy, soft green foliage. 18–24". Prefers deep to light shade, rich, moist, well-drained soil, and moisture throughout the growing season. Plant in the spring.

### Athyrium filix-femina (Lady fern)

Deep-cut, bright yellow-green foliage. 24–48". Prefers partial shade and moisture throughout growing season. Plant in the spring.

### Athyrium goeringianum 'Pictum' (Japanese painted fern)

Coarse gray-green and red foliage. 12". Prefers partial shade, as sun leaches out color. Needs enriched soil with considerable amounts of organic matter worked in. Water regularly during growing season. Plant in the spring.

### Dennstaedtia (Hay-scented fern) 🦌

Green, elegant, arching fronds. 20–32". Fragrant when crushed. Thrives in moisture in sun or shade. Is not fussy about soil. Excellent for naturalizing but not good for small gardens because of rampant growth habit.

### Matteuccia struthiopteris (Ostrich fern) 🦌

Yellow-green, feathery fronds. 3–6'. Prefers deep to light shade. Needs enriched soil with considerable amounts of organic matter worked in. Water regularly during growing season. Plant in the spring.

### Osmunda cinnamomea (Cinnamon fern) 🦌

Native fern with deep-green, waxy textured fronds on cinnamon-colored stalks. 3–4'. Prefers deep to light shade. Needs enriched soil with considerable amounts of organic matter worked in. Water regularly during growing season. Plant in the spring.

### Osmunda regalis (Royal fern) 🦌

Native fern with deep forest-green fronds. 4–6'. Prefers deep to light shade and slightly acidic soil. Water regularly during growing season. Plant in the spring.

Ostrich fern

Maidenhair fern

Lady fern

*Polypodium virginianum* (American wall fern)
Dark green, low-spreading, evergreen frond stalks. Prefers partial shade and well-drained soil. Use as ground cover.

*Thelypteris hexagonoptera* (Beech fern)
Deciduous fern with bright green frond. Thrives in shade and acid soils. Use as ground cover for shady places.

# Grasses

Bloom times refer to peak time for plumy panicles or seed heads, not for blossoms, as grass does not sport bloom. All cultivars included are perennials and hardy throughout the United States unless otherwise indicated.

*Cortaderia selloana* 'Pumila' (Compact pampas grass) 🦌
Ornamental grass. Silky panicles on tall bluish clumps. 4–6'. Thrives in full sun. Provide moisture during extended summer drought until established. Hardy to Zone 7. Plant in the spring or fall. Cut foliage to ground before spring growth commences.

*Festuca* (Fescue grass) 🦌
Ornamental grass for massing. Grows in tufts to about 8". Prefers dry conditions once established but should be watered regularly during prolonged summer drought, as roots like moisture. Plant in the spring. Cut foliage to ground before spring growth commences. Many varieties are available, and some make good ground covers.

*Holcus lanatus* 'Variegatus' (Variegated velvet grass) 🦋 🦌
Ornamental grass for massing. Green and white variegated leaves. 8". Tolerates sandy soil. Drought resistant once established. Cut foliage to the ground before spring growth commences. Can be grown as a ground cover.

*Imperata cylindrica rubra* (Japanese bloodgrass) 🦌
Ornamental, open-spreading grass. Erect, pointed foliage

with red tips. 12–24". Plant in partial shade for most leaf color. Tolerates poor soil and dry spells but should be watered regularly during prolonged summer drought. Plant in the spring. Cut foliage to ground before spring growth commences. Not hardy north of Zone 7.

### Miscanthus ꙮ

A large group of ornamental grasses. Broad grassy foliage with silvery tan plumes in midsummer. 4–7'. Prefers partial shade but tolerates full sun. Tolerates dry spells but should be watered regularly during prolonged summer drought. Plant in the spring or fall. Cut foliage to ground before spring growth commences. Useful species include *M. saccariflorus* (silver banner grass), *M. sinensis* 'Gracillimus' (maiden grass), and *M. sinensis* 'Zebrinus' (zebra grass).

### Panicum virgatum (Switch grass) ꙮ

Ornamental grass. Finely cut green foliage. 4–7'. Delicate cloudlike blooms from midsummer to fall. Prefers full sun. Water regularly as roots prefer moisture. Plant in the spring or fall. Cut foliage to ground before spring growth commences. Bloom persists through winter and adds interesting touch to winter landscape. Some varieties that have leaves that turn a beautiful red in the fall are 'Rehbraun,' 'Rostrahlbusch,' and 'Rubrum.'

### Pennisetum alopecuroides (Fountain grass) ꙮ

Ornamental grass. Very fine arching foliage. 3–4'. Rose-tan, foxtail-shaped bloom from midsummer through fall. Prefers full sun and sandy soil. Tolerates dry spells but should be watered regularly during prolonged summer drought. Plant in the spring. Cut foliage to ground before spring growth commences. Not hardy north of Zone 6. *Pennisetum rubrum* is a tender grass that is enjoying great popularity these days. Foliage is red. However, it is an annual and will not winter over in most parts of the country.

Maiden grass

Variegated velvet grass

Fountain grass

## Ground Covers

Many traditional ground covers are suitable for rock gardens or for planting in rock ledge areas. These plants are perennials unless otherwise noted.

*Achillea tomentosa* (Woolly yarrow) ❀ ❦
Yellow, tightly structured flower heads on fernlike foliage. 3". Thrives in enriched, sandy soil in full sun. Drought resistant once established. Deadhead spent blooms to encourage repeat bloom.

*Ajuga* (Bugleweed) ❀ ❦
Blue, purple, or white blossoms on vigorous, semi-evergreen plants with dark-green, burgundy, bronze-purple, or variegated foliage, depending on variety. 4–10". Thrives in full sun or partial shade. If you wish a less vigorous cultivar to use in a garden scheme, select *A. genevensis* (Geneva bugle).

*Alyssum saxatile*, see *Aurinia saxatilis*

*Arabis caucasica* (Rock cress)
White or rose-pink clusters of blossoms over silver-green tufted foliage. 12". Thrives in gritty, well-drained sandy soil in full sun. Plant in the fall. One of the earliest blooming perennials, well-suited to a rock garden or border as well.

*Arenaria verna* 'Caespitosa' (Moss sandwort) ❀
Spring-blooming, white, starlike blossoms on delicate, mosslike foliage. Thrives in full sun or partial shade. Ideal for tucking into wall cracks or between stepping stones.

*Armeria maritima* (Thrift) ❀
White or deep-rose blossoms on semievergreen foliage. 4". Thrives in sandy soil in full sun or partial shade. Easy to propagate. Divide after bloom and replant.

*Aurinia saxatilis* (Gold dust, basket of gold) ❀ ❦
Brilliant sulfur-gold clusters of blossoms in the spring, on sil-

Pachysandra

Lamb's ear

Lamium

145

very gray foliage. 6". Prefers full sun. Plant in early spring. Usually sold as *Alyssum saxatile*. 'Citrina' is a pale yellow version, more subtle than the brilliant yellow varieties.

### *Calluna vulgaris* (Heather) 🦌

Tiny white, pink, or red blossoms on spikes in the summer or fall on evergreen foliage. 18". Thrives in poor soil in full sun. In partial shade bloom will be less profuse. Needs some moisture.

### *Cerastium tomentosum* (Snow-in-summer) ❁

White blossoms in June on woolly gray foliage. 6–10". Thrives in poor soil and in full sun.

### *Ceratostigma plumbaginoides* (Blue plumbago) ❁

Stunning deep-blue blossoms in late August through late fall on glossy deep-green foliage that turns bronze in cold weather. 6–12". Thrives in full sun or light shade. Can become weedy if not contained.

### *Cotoneaster,* see Shrubs

### *Epimedium* (Barrenwort) ❁ 🦌

Rose, yellow, orange or white blossoms in clusters over deep-green dense foliage, often evergreen. 1'. Thrives in light shade in deep, rich soil. Will also grow reasonably well in full sun or deep shade. Tolerates root competition under trees. Is not invasive. Perhaps the most elegant and the most effective of all ground covers.

### *Erica carnea* (Spring heath) 🦌

Spring-blooming cousin of heather, with red, pink, or white spikes of blossoms on evergreen foliage. 18". Thrives in poor soil in full sun. In partial shade bloom will be less profuse. Needs some moisture.

### *Euonymus fortunei* (Winter creeper) ❁

Deep-green evergreen foliage with pale red fruit in the summer and fall. Thrives in full sun or partial shade and in poor soil. Look for low-growing varieties, many of which have variegated foliage in white, pink, or yellow.

### *Festuca,* see Grasses

### *Gallium odorata,* see Herbs

### *Hedera helix* (English ivy) ❁

Ivy, grown for its handsome foliage, which ranges from deep-green to yellow or white variegations, depending on the variety chosen, can be trained either as a vine or a ground cover. Thrives in full sun or deep shade and once established is drought resistant. Prune every fall to keep in bounds.

### *Holcus lanatus* 'Variegatus,' see Grasses

### *Hypericum calycinum* (Saint-John's-wort) ❁

Big bright yellow blossoms in late summer on medium-green foliage. 6". Thrives in full sun and in sandy soil. Foliage turns purplish in the fall.

### *Iberis sempervirens* (Candytuft) ❁ 🦌

Clusters of white blossoms on lustrous, needlelike evergreen foliage. 6–24". Thrives in full sun. Many improved varieties now available. The dwarf *Iberis saxatilis* (rock candytuft) is particularly attractive.

### *Lamium maculatum* (Dead nettle) ❁ 🦌

Clusters of white blossoms on a plant grown mostly for its silvery-white and green variegated foliage. 12". Thrives in light shade. Particularly attractive is *Lamium maculatum* 'White Nancy.'

### *Liriope spicata* (Creeping lilyturf) ❁

Lilac to white blossoms on spikes in mid- to late summer on green grasslike foliage. 8–12". Thrives in full sun or partial shade. To propagate, divide in the spring and space plants 2–3" apart.

*Pachysandra terminalis* 🦌
White blossom in the spring on deep glossy green or variegated foliage. Prefers partial shade or deep shade. Propagates easily from cuttings or from unearthed, unwanted stock. Just wrap roots around finger and plant.

*Phlox divaricata* (Wild blue phlox)
Lovely blue or lavender blossoms in the spring on medium-green leaf clusters. Prefers partial shade and needs moisture. Spreading stems put down roots.

*Phlox subulata* (Moss pink) 🐝
Small white, pink, or pale blue clusters of blossoms in mid-spring on matlike, semievergreen foliage. 6". Thrives in full sun or partial shade. Drought resistant once established. A better choice than *Phlox stolonifera*, with many new varieties in clean colors available.

*Polemonium caeruleum* (Jacob's ladder) 🐝 🦌
Small cup-shaped blue or white blossoms in mid- to late spring on delicate medium-green mounds of foliage. To 14". Thrives in either sun or shade. Drought resistant once established. Plant in the spring only. 'Blue Pearl' and 'Album' are recommended varieties.

*Polypodium virginianum*, see Ferns

*Sedum* (Stonecrop) 🐝 🌱
Scores of varieties with white, pink, yellow, gold, red, or blue blossoms on jade-green, yellow, purple, red, or gray succulent foliage. Prefers full sun. Plant at any time during the season. A few varieties are invasive. *Sedum spectabile* 'Autumn Joy', the most spectacular cultivar, sports large mauve-pink flower heads that turn brilliant rust in the fall on succulent, jade-green foliage. To 36". Research into available varieties is well worth the effort for some are exquisite.

*Sempervivum* (Hens and chickens) 🐝
The perfect companion for sedums offers elegant rosettes of succulent foliage in reds, greens, and blue-grays. Stalks of bizarre blossoms emerge in early summer. Prefers full sun. Research into available varieties is worth the effort. Echeveria is another large species that includes cultivars with the common name hens and chickens that are useful as ground covers or in the rock garden.

*Stachys byzantina*, see Herbs

*Thelypteris hexagonoptera*, see Ferns

*Thymus*, see Herbs

*Veronica* (Speedwell) 🐝
There are many varieties of veronica, but only a few can be grown as ground covers. Most offer purple, white, pink, or blue blossoms on pale-green or deep-green foliage. Prefers full sun. Drought resistant once established. *Veronica allioni* has spikes of purple blossoms over leathery deep-green foliage. 4". *V. filiformis*, the familiar lawn pest, with small pale blue blossoms on dense mats of medium-green foliage, is very invasive. Taller growing varieties are not appropriate for use as ground covers.

*Vinca minor* (Periwinkle, creeping myrtle) 🐝
This familiar ground cover has medium-blue or white blossoms on attractive glossy green foliage. 6". A very versatile plant in terms of adapting to the environment, it thrives in full sun, partial shade, or deep shade. Can be invasive if conditions are ideal.

# Herbs

Since most herbs are native to the dry areas of the Mediterranean and Middle East, where either sandy or very poor soil is the rule, they are an excellent choice for a low-maintenance country garden. All cultivars included in this list are perennials and hardy throughout North America, except for the far northern reaches of Canada, unless otherwise indicated.

### *Allium sativum* (Garlic) ✿ 🦌

Bulb. Hardy, jade-green, spearlike foliage sporting purple clusters of blossoms in midsummer. To 36". Prefers full sun and well-drained soil. Plant bulbs in the spring or fall. You can simply plant cloves of store-bought garlic. Elephant garlic, the giant, milder version is available through mail-order sources. For larger bulbs, remove flower heads. In August, dig bulbs, clean them, and hang them by their necks in a dry place out of the sun until the foliage is dry. Store bulbs in a refrigerator. Individual cloves also can be replanted after digging for the next year's crop.

### *Allium schoenoprasum* (Chive) ✿ 🦌

Rhizome. Medium-green clumps of spearlike foliage sporting clusters of lavender blossoms in the spring. 12". Prefers full sun and well-drained soil. Plant from seed anytime during the growing season. Chive self-seeds, so to avoid unwanted plants, deadhead blossoms after flowering. An easily grown, indispensable kitchen herb, which is being used more and more for decorative landscape purposes.

### *Anethum graveolens* (Dill) ✿

Annual. Feathery, medium-green foliage sporting seed heads of yellowish blossoms. To 36". Prefers full sun and well-drained soil. Plant from seed in the spring after all danger of frost, and then again every three weeks for successive crops. An easily grown, indispensable kitchen herb. Feathery foliage can be worked into the landscape scheme nicely.

### *Artemisia dranunculus* (French tarragon) ✿ 🦌

Perennial. Medium-green, glossy foliage. 12–36". Prefers full sun and poor soil and resents water. Plant in the spring after all danger of frost. Carefree once established and handy in the kitchen.

### *Chamaemelum nobile* (Chamomile)

Perennial. Low-growing, spreading plant with bright green,

Lavender 'Hidcote'

Sage

soft-textured foliage. To 6". Small, white-petaled, daisylike blossoms from late spring through summer. Apple-scented foliage. Thrives in sun to partial shade in well-drained soil. Water regularly during prolonged summer drought. A good selection for planting in walkways. Leaves can be dried and used to brew a refreshing tea.

### Gallium odoratum (Sweet woodruff)

Perennial. Narrow, bright-green, aromatic foliage, with small white flowers in late spring and summer. 6–12". Thrives in shade in enriched soil. Requires regular moisture. Plant in the spring after all danger of frost. Dried leaves can be used to flavor white wine. May wine is flavored with this herb. Very useful as a ground cover in shady areas.

### Lavandula (Lavender) ❀ ❦

Perennial. Narrow, silvery-gray foliage, with white, pink, or lavender spikes of tiny blossoms. 6–48". Prefers full sun. Plant in the spring after all danger of frost or in the fall. Among the varieties recommended are low-growing varieties of *Lavandula angustifolia*, including 'Hidcote' (12"), 'Munstead' (18"), and 'Compact' (10"). To keep plant tidy, shear after flowering.

### Menthe (Mint) ❀

Perennial. Beyond the familiar mint-flavored varieties, there are also mints with apple, pineapple, orange, lemon, and spearmint flavors. Foliage is deep green, jade-green, or purplish with some varieties variegated in cream or yellow. Thrives in full sun. Plant in the spring after all danger of frost. Mint can become invasive if happy. Plant it in containers that are sunk into the earth to keep it from wandering.

### Nepeta (Catnip, catmint) ❀

Perennial. Tiny blue, lavender, yellow, or white sprays of tubular blossoms on medium-green foliage. 12–24". Thrives in well-drained soil in full sun. Plant outdoors anytime during the growing season. Catnip is an ideal border or edging plant unless you have a cat. An intoxicated cat can obliterate a planting in no time flat.

### Ocimum basilicum (Basil)

Annual. The familiar kitchen herb, with foliage in deep green, bronze, or purplish green. 12–36". Prefers full sun and requires watering throughout season. Plant in situ in the spring after all danger of frost. Look for new varieties, some dwarf and moundlike, many with purple or bronze foliage, and use in plantings for color effects.

### Origanum vulgare (Oregano) ❦

Perennial. Small, medium-green heart-shaped foliage. 24–30". Some varieties have a sprawling growth habit. Greek oregano (*Origanum heracleoticum*) is neater and more pungent. Thrives in full sun and in well-drained, enriched soil and requires water throughout the season. Divide plants every three years to maintain vigor. Related to the annual marjoram, *O. majorana*.

### Salvia officinalis (Sage) ❀ ❦

Perennial. Bright-green or deep-burgundy quilted foliage with lovely violet blossoms in tiered clusters in mid- to late spring. To 36". Thrives in full sun. Plant in the spring after all danger of frost. Excellent for foliage color accents in borders. Select *Salvia officinalis* 'Purpurascens' for purplish tones and 'Tricolor' for variegated white, which, because it is tinged with purple, appears pink.

### Santolina chamaecyparissus (Lavender cotton) ❀

Perennial. Silver-gray foliage, sporting miniature golden buttonlike blossoms in early summer. To 18". Prefers full sun and enriched soil. Will also grow in partial shade. Plant in the spring after all danger of frost. Prune each spring to encourage vigorous growth during season. Do not cut to ground in the fall as new foliage grows on old wood. Divide ever three years to keep plant vigorous. In cooler climates, mulch plants late in the fall and uncover them in early spring.

### Stachys byzantina (Lamb's ear) ❀ ❦

Perennial. Low mat of woolly, silver white foliage. To 6". Flower stalks are unattractive. Prefers full sun and well-drained soil. Also thrives in partial shade. Plant in the spring after all danger of frost or in the fall. Divide every two years for more. Some gardeners remove the flower stalks. A beautiful plant that can be used either as a ground cover or an accent in beds. Look for the new bloomless variety: no flower stalks, and leaves are larger than the common lamb's ears.

### Thymus (Thyme)

Perennial. Many varieties of low-growing, matlike plants in bright green and bluish gray, with silver, yellow, or white variegations, sporting tiny flowers in pink, purple, white, or rose, depending on variety. Prefers full sun but will thrive in partial shade. Drought tolerant, but results are better with regular watering. Plant in the spring after all danger of frost or transplant rooted cuttings throughout the season. Shear each fall to maintain vigor. Recommended varieties include:

Thymus X citriodorus (Lemon thyme): Distinct lemon scent with green foliage and rose-lavender blossoms. 'Aureus' has bright green leaves edged in cream; 'Argenteus' has gray-green leaves edged in white. 4–12"

T. herba-barona (Caraway-scented thyme): Narrow foliage with rose-pink blossoms. 2–5".

T. praecox arcticus (Mother-of-thyme): Matlike dark green foliage with white or purple blossoms. To 4".

T. pseudolanuginosus (Woolly thyme): Matlike gray woolly foliage with pink blossoms. 1'.

T. vulgaris (Garden thyme): Spreading mounds with gray-green leaves. 6–15".

T. vulgaris 'Argenteus' (Silver thyme): Silver-white variegated foliage. 6–15".

## Perennials

All of the entries included are hardy as far north as Zone 5, with many hardy to Zones 3 and 4.

### Achillea (Yarrow) ✿ ❦

Yellow, white, pink, and red flower clusters on erect stalks with fernlike foliage. 24–48". Thrives in full sun. Plant outdoors in the spring or fall. Flowers are excellent for drying.

### Aconitum (Monkshood)

Dark blue or blue-and-white spires of blossoms on 3–4' stalks. Dark green, leafy foliage. Thrives in enriched soil in partial shade or full sun. Needs moisture. Plant outdoors in mid-spring. Plant increases slowly and once established resents being moved. Monkshood is a good substitute for delphiniums if they are difficult in your area.

### Alchemilla (Lady's mantle)

Tiny chartreuse clusters of flowers on 12–18" stalks. Pleated, gray-green, rounded leaves. Thrives in partial shade or full sun. Needs moisture. Plant outdoors in mid-spring. Propagate by division.

### Amsonia tabernaemontana (Bluestar) ❦

True-blue clusters of upright or drooping blossoms and delicate, willowlike foliage. 12–36". Thrives in enriched soil in partial shade or shade. Needs moisture. Plant outdoors in mid-spring. Cut plants to ground after killing frost. Pruning after bloom helps maintain foliage, which turns a brilliant yellow in the fall.

### Anemone X hybrida (Japanese anemone)

Pink, rose, or white blossoms with yellow centers. Medium-green foliage. 18–48", depending on variety. Thrives in moderately fertile soil in partial shade or full sun. Needs moisture. Plant outdoors in mid-spring or fall. Cut plants to ground after killing frost. Because they are late bloomers, Japanese anemones are particularly useful in the garden. Blossoms are delicate in appearance, which is rare for cultivars that bloom in the fall. Often sold as Anemone japonica.

### Anemone pulsatilla (Pasqueflower) ✿

Pale purple, white, or deep red cuplike blossoms and feathery, hirsute pale green foliage. 10–12". Thrives in partial shade. Drought resistant in cool climates. Plant outdoors in the spring or fall. After bloom, stunning clematislike seed heads cover the plant. Propagate from root cuttings.

### Anthemis tinctoria (Golden marguerite) ❧

Yellow, daisylike blossoms and gray-green, finely cut foliage. 18–24". Thrives in full sun. Plant outdoors in mid-spring or fall. Deadhead throughout summer and fall to prolong blooming. Provides masses of flowers during the summer. In Tudor England, anthemis was used for lawns, and when it was mowed, its fragrance, similar to chamomile, filled the air.

### Aquilegia (Columbine) ❧ ❧

Delicate, trumpetlike flowers in a full range of colors on often feathery, fernlike foliage. 18–36". Thrives in enriched soil in full sun or partial shade. Needs moisture. Plant outdoors in mid-spring or fall. Cut foliage to ground after killing frost. Delicate blossoms enhance the spring garden. Blue varieties are particularly beautiful.

### Artemisia (Perennial dusty miller) ❧ ❧

Grown for silvery gray foliage. 12–36", depending on variety. Thrives in enriched, well-drained, sandy soil in full sun. Plant outdoors in mid-spring or late summer.

### Aruncus dioicus (Goatsbeard) ❧

Cream, plumelike blossoms, similar to astilbe, on medium-green, serrated foliage. 4–6'. Thrives in moisture-retentive soil in light shade. Plant outdoors in mid-spring or fall. Treat as an herbaceous shrub. The plant is too large for the average perennial border or bed. Self-seeds but not invasively.

### Asclepia tuberosa (Orange butterfly weed, butterfly milkweed) ❧ ❧ ❧

Bright orange umbrels of flowers in midsummer on bright-green foliage. To 36". Thrives in full sun and sandy soil. Plants are late to break dormancy, so care must be taken not to dig them up mistakenly in the spring. *Asclepia incarnata*, a less familiar native, has pink and white flowers.

### Aster (Michaelmas daisy)

A large group of perennial asters in purple, white, pink, blue or red on gray-green leaves. 6"–6', depending on variety. Thrives in full sun to partial shade in moderately fertile soil. Dislikes very hot climates, thriving in cool, moist conditions. Plant in late spring or early fall. Propagate by dividing, taking small divisions from the outside of the clumps.

### Astilbe ❧

White, pink, red, rose, peach, or apricot feathery plumes of blossoms on sturdy, medium-green foliage. 12–30". Thrives in moderately enriched soil in partial shade or full sun. Needs moisture. Plant outdoors in mid-spring or fall. Remove spent blossoms after bloom cycle. Provides soft, feathery texture to the landscape.

### Baptisia australis (Blue wild indigo) ❧ ❧

Indigo blue spikes of pealike blossoms on 3–4' stalks over gray-green foliage. 3–4'. Thrives in enriched soil in full sun. Will grow in partial shade but requires staking as plant can become rangy. Plant outdoors in mid-spring or fall.

### Brunnera macrophylla (Forget-me-not) ❧

Sky blue, tiny forget-me-not-like blossoms on handsome medium-green, heart-shaped foliage. 12–18". Thrives in moderately fertile soil in partial or deep shade. Plant outdoors in mid-spring or fall. One of the few perennials that will thrive beneath the extensive surface root system of maples and beeches.

### Campanula (Bellflower) ❧ ❧

A very large family of flowering perennials, including *Campanula carpatica*, *C. glomerata*, and *C. persicifolia*. Purple, pink, lavender, blue or white clusters of upward-facing, bell-shaped or star-shaped flowers on deep-green foliage. 6"–3½'. Thrives in moderately fertile, moist, but well-drained soil in partial shade. For best results, mulch roots during the hot summer months.

*Centaurea macrocephala* (Globe centaurea) ❀
Large bright yellow thistlelike flowers on medium-green handsome foliage. 4'. Not fussy about soil, prefers full sun and is easy to grow. Very hardy and not invasive. But be sure to deadhead as plant will self-sow prolifically.

*Centranthus ruber* (Red valerian)
Pink, white, or reddish clusters of flowers on medium-green foliage. 2–3'. Not fussy about soil. Thrives in full sun. Somewhat short lived in hotter climates. For a second bloom, cut back after first bloom.

*Chrysanthemum coccineum* (Painted daisy) ⚘
Daisylike blossoms in white, pink, red, and combinations thereof on medium-green foliage. 24". Thrives in moderately fertile soil in full sun or partial shade. Needs moisture. Plant outdoors in mid-spring or fall. Deadhead after bloom to encourage second bloom. Another carefree, easy-to-grow perennial.

*Chrysanthemum maximum* (Shasta daisy)
White with yellow centered, daisylike single or double blossoms on handsome deep-green foliage. 12–42". Thrives in moderately fertile soil in full sun or partial shade. Needs moisture. Plant outdoors in mid-spring or fall. Deadhead after bloom to encourage second bloom. A wide variety is available from dwarfs to giants, some with small flowers, some with large.

*Chrysanthemum* X *morifolium* (Chrysanthemum) ❀ ⚘
Fall-blooming plant in wide range of colors, including yellow, gold, white, rust, orange, red, purple, and lavender. Many blossom shapes, but pompon is perhaps the most readily available. Medium-green compact foliage, depending on variety. 8–36". Thrives in moderately fertile soil in full sun but will tolerate semishade. Plant outdoors in mid-spring. Cut back foliage after killing frost. The following spring, dig plant, divide, discard woody center, and replant divisions. After planting, pinch shoots every three weeks until July 4 to encourage branching and thus more bloom.

*Chrysopsis* (Golden aster) ❀
Yellow, daisylike 2" blossoms. 3–4'. Thrives in sandy soil in full sun. Plant outdoors in mid-spring or fall. Cut back to ground after frost.

*Cimicifuga* (Bugbane, snakeroot) ⚘
White spires of flowers on handsome green foliage. 4–6'. Prefers moist soil in a shady location. Foliage has a very unpleasant odor that repels insects (hence, bugbane), but you must get very close to the plant to smell it. Cimicifuga can be rampantly invasive, but it is useful in the back of the border.

*Coreopsis* ❀ ⚘ ⚘
Yellow and yellow-mahogany-red, daisylike blossoms on medium-green, handsome foliage. 24". Thrives in poor soil in full sun. Plant outdoors in mid-spring or fall. Very easy to grow. If you want a lot of carefree yellow flowers, this is a good choice.

*Corydalis lutea* ❀
Clusters of yellow blossoms on gray foliage. 15". Is not fussy about soil and self-seeds when happy. Thrives in full sun or partial to deep shade. Plant in mid-spring or early fall. Spreads but can be contained.

*Delphinium*
Spikes of florets in white, blue, purple, pink, and combinations thereof on loose, medium-green foliage, depending on variety. 2–7', depending on variety. Thrives in very rich soil in full sun or partial shade. Needs moisture. Plant outdoors in mid-spring or fall, but spring is best. Taller varieties require staking. Remove flower heads after bloom and plant may bloom again in the fall. Can be difficult to grow unless conditions are ideal, but because of their spectacular beauty in arrangements well worth the effort. If you do not have luck with delphiniums, substitute easy-to-grow annual larkspur, which, although not as spectacular, will create a similar vertical effect in the garden.

*Dianthus* (Pinks) ✹ ⍋ 🦌

Single or double, carnation-type blossoms in white, pink, red, or combinations thereof, on elegant, blue-green or gray-green foliage, depending on variety. 8–18". Thrives in sandy soil in full sun or partial shade. Plant outdoors in mid-spring or fall. Deadhead after bloom to keep plant tidy. All pinks offer a lovely clovelike fragrance.

*Dicentra spectabilis* (Bleeding heart) 🦌

Pink or white heart-shaped blossoms on graceful, arching stems over medium-green foliage. 12–36". Thrives in moderately fertile soil in partial shade. Needs moisture. Plant outdoors in the spring. Remove branches of spent blossoms after bloom to keep plant tidy. Foliage withers toward the end of summer, so an overplanting of annuals in the garden is recommended. Blooms in tandem with tulips, azaleas, and dogwood. Adds a graceful elegance to the spring garden.

*Digitalis grandiflora* (Foxglove)

All colors except blue. Spikes of pitcher-shaped florets on long stalks over medium-green rosettes of foliage, depending on variety. 1–5'. Thrives in well-drained soil in partial shade or full sun. Needs moisture. Since foxglove is a biennial, start outdoors from seed after all danger of frost. Plant will not bloom first year but will winter over and bloom second year. Once established, deadhead after bloom for possible rebloom. Easily grown from seed, foxglove may perennialize. If not, treat it as a biennial.

*Doronicum caucasicum* (Leopard's bane)

Yellow, daisylike blossoms on handsome deep-green foliage. 20". Thrives in full sun or partial shade. Needs moisture. Plant outdoors in mid-spring or fall. Deadhead after bloom. Plant becomes semidormant after bloom, so overplant with annuals in May or June. An early-blooming perennial used to soften spring bulb plantings.

*Echinacea* (Purple coneflower) ✹ ⍋ 🦌

Plum-pink or white daisylike 3" blossoms with orange cone

Monarda

Aruncus

Ajuga

Kniphofia

Phlox

Iris siberica

centers on handsome deep-green foliage. 3'. Thrives in sandy soil in full sun. Plant outdoors in mid-spring or fall. Deadhead spent blooms to encourage second bloom. One of the easiest perennials to grow.

### *Echinops* (Globe thistle) 🌿 🍸 🦌

Steel blue thistlelike blossoms on large-leafed, gray-green, hirsute foliage. 2–4'. Thrives in well-drained soil in full sun. Plant outdoors in mid-spring or fall. Divide plant only after three years.

### *Eryngium* (Sea holly)

Steel blue lacy thistlelike blooms on thorny, hirsute foliage. 18–36". Thrives in enriched soil in full sun. Needs moisture. Plant outdoors in mid-spring or fall. Deadhead after bloom. Taller varieties may need staking. Bizarre looking blossoms add interesting touches to summer gardens.

### *Eupatorium coelestinum* (Hardy ageratum)

Fluffy pale purple blossoms resembling annual ageratum on coarse, hairy foliage. 36". Thrives in well-drained soil in full or partial sun. Needs moisture. Plant outdoors in mid-spring or fall. Plant benefits from pinching during season. This encourages sturdy branching and eliminates need for staking.

### *Eupatorium purpureum* (Joe-Pye weed)

Purplish pink clusters of flowers on large-leafed, deep-green foliage. 6'. Thrives in full sun. Needs moisture, growing vigorously in boglike environments. Plant outdoors in the spring or fall. Impressive plants useful in the back of the border.

### *Euphorbia epthymoides* (Cushion spurge)

Bright yellow, chartreuse, and green clusters of florets and leaves combine over bright-green foliage. 12–18". Thrives in full sun. Needs moisture. Plant outdoors in mid-spring or fall. Remove dead foliage after killing frost. Sap of plant is irritating to sensitive skin, causing a rash, but it will not cause illness.

### *Filipendula rubra* (Queen-of-the-prairie) 🦌

Soft pink clusters of tiny flowers form fluffy plumes over large, deep-green leaves. 4–7'. May need staking in windy areas. Thrives in full sun. Needs moisture. Plant outdoors in mid-spring or fall. Does not do well in very hot, very dry climates. The blossoms are utterly breathtaking. Not as fussy as equally spectacular delphiniums, which also do not like hot, dry climates, so any fussing is worth every minute.

### *Gaillardia* (Blanket flower) 🌿

Yellow, red, or bicolored daisylike blossoms on handsome medium-green foliage. 12–24". Thrives in full sun. Plant outdoors in mid-spring or fall. Deadhead after bloom to keep plant tidy and to encourage more flowers.

### *Geranium* (Cranesbill or hardy geranium)

This group of plants is not in any way related to the annual bright red geraniums (pelargonium) that, for better or for worse, fill the window boxes of the earth. They are a separate species, hardy, a fine plant that is available in a wide range of varieties. Pink, deep-blue, white, violet, and magenta five-petaled blossoms on attractive, cut-leaved foliage. 6–18", depending on variety. Thrives in well-drained soil in light shade. Plant outdoors in mid-spring or fall. Easily propagated without lifting the clump. Push your fingers down among the roots and separate a piece from the parent plant.

### *Geum* 🦌

Orange, red, or yellow blossoms on deep-green foliage. 1–2'. Thrives in well-drained soil in sun or semishade. Plant outdoors in mid-spring or fall. Stunning when interplanted with purple or blue blooming perennials such as brunnera and forget-me-not.

### *Gypsophila* (Baby's Breath) 🦌

White or pink sprays of tiny flowers on bushlike, graceful plants, depending on variety. 6"–3', depending on variety. Thrives in well-drained, fertile, alkaline soil in full sun. Needs moisture. Plant outdoors in mid-spring or fall.

Remove dead foliage after frost. Adds soft cloudlike quality to a perennial planting.

## Helenium autumnale (Sneezeweed)

Yellow, orange, mahogany disklike flowers with reflexed petals on handsome bright-green foliage. 2–5'. Thrives in full sun in moist soil. Plant outdoors in mid-spring or fall. Pinch plants from mid-spring until midsummer to keep plants vigorous. Divide clumps ever third year.

## Heliopsis helianthoides (Sunflower) ✣ ⚘

Golden yellow, double, pompon-shaped blossoms on medium-green foliage. 3–4'. Thrives in full sun. Plant outdoors in mid-spring or fall. Deadhead after bloom to encourage second bloom.

## Helleborus (Chrismas or Lenten rose) ✣ ⚘

Green, white, or pink 2" blossoms on glossy palm-shaped foliage. 1–3'. Thrives in rich soil in partial shade. Plant outdoors in mid-spring or fall. One of the earliest blooming of all perennials, providing welcome relief from the mid- to late-winter doldrums.

## Hemerocallis (Daylily) ✣

The familiar lily blossoms over straplike medium-green foliage. 12–48". Thrives in full sun or partial shade. Plant outdoors in mid-spring or fall. Foolproof and available in hundreds of varieties and colors to suit every landscape.

## Heuchera sanginea (Coralbells) ✣

Red, pink, or white spikes of small, bell-shaped blossoms over clustered medium-green or variegated foliage. 12–18". Thrives in moderately fertile, dry soil in full sun or partial shade. Plant outdoors in mid-spring or fall. Deadhead after bloom to keep plant tidy. Like baby's breath, the small florets of coralbells are useful in softening the perennial garden.

## Hibiscus moscheutos (Rose mallow)

Flamboyant pink, white, rose, fire engine red, and combinations thereof, 7–10" blossoms over stunning lobed foliage. 3–6'. Thrives in enriched, well-drained soil in full sun. Tolerates bog conditions and clay soil. Plant in mid-spring, not in the fall. Rose mallow is really a small shrub, although classified as an herbaceous perennial. If you want to make a startling statement in your garden, this plant is for you. *Hibiscus moscheutos* subs. *palustris* (marsh mallow), native to East Coast bogs, is pink.

## Hosta (Plaintain lily)

White, lilac, or pale lavender delicate blossom spikes on lush foliage from several inches to 4', in colors ranging from yellow to dark green, gray and near steel blue, often edged or speckled with white, cream, or yellow. Leaves can be smooth, ribbed, or quilted. 2–36". Hosta will grow in just about any kind of soil and light conditions but thrives in partial shade in enriched, moist soil. Plant outdoors in mid-spring or fall. Remove spent blossoms after bloom to keep plant tidy. Hosta is an indispensable foliage plant. I favor 'Honeybells' (*Hosta plantaginea* X *H. lancifolis*), which has a light pleasing honeysuckle scent.

## Iris kaempferi (Japanese iris)

Blue-purple, white, or yellow and combinations thereof. Spear-shaped, medium-green foliage. To 24". Thrives in wet soil in full sun but will tolerate partial shade. Plant outdoor in the spring or fall. Many cultivars available. The closely related *Iris laevigata* is a true bog plant and may perform even better in very wet soils. Adapts to wetland conditions.

## Iris pseudacorus (Yellow flag iris)

Light yellow to orange flowers over spear-shaped, medium-green foliage. To 5'. Naturalized on the East Coast and found in wet areas. Thrives in full sun but will tolerate partial shade. Plant outdoors in the spring or fall. Various cultivars available. Adapts to wetland conditions.

## Iris siberica (Siberian iris) ✣

Blue, purple, white, or yellow and combinations thereof.

Spear-shaped, medium-green foliage. 18–36". Thrives in well-drained soil in full sun but will tolerate partial shade. Plant outdoors in mid-spring or fall. Do not deadhead spent stalks as dried pods are attractive in the fall garden.

### *Iris*, tall bearded 🐛
The familiar bearded iris comes in a remarkable array of colors and heights. Foliage is jade-green, spearlike, and remains attractive throughout the season. Thrives in enriched, well-drained soil in full sun but will tolerate partial shade. Mid-summer is the best time to plant bearded iris but the fall will do. Remove spent stalks after bloom. Divide and replant every three to five years, depending on vigor of plant. Recent additions to the iris family include re-bloomers, that is, plants that bloom in the spring and also in the fall. To assure fall bloom, remove all stalks after bloom.

### *Kniphofia* (Torch flower) 🐛
Red and yellow pokerlike blooms over gray-green grasslike foliage. 18–36". Thrives in well-drained or sandy soil in full sun. Plant outdoors in mid-spring. Deadhead through season and shear foliage when it becomes rangy. Torch flower adds a tropical touch to a country garden.

### *Liatris* (Gay-feather or blazing star) 🦌
Rosy-purple or white whiskerlike blossoms on spear-shaped basal leaves, large at the bottom of the stalk, diminishing in size to the top of the stalk. 3–6'. Flowers on spikes bloom from the top down.

### *Ligularia* or *Senecio* (Ragwort)
Flamboyant yellow or orange spikes of florets over leathery heart-shaped leaves. 3–6", depending on variety. Thrives in semishade in moist, rich soil. Cannot survive drought. Foliage will wilt in hot sun even if roots are moist, but this is nothing to be concerned about. A splendid plant for boglike conditions or edging a water garden.

### *Linum* (Flax) 🐛
Sky blue or white small blossoms on willowy stems. 12–18". Thrives in enriched, well-drained, soil in full sun. Plant outdoors in mid-spring. Easy to grow from seed. Sow in situ in mid-spring. Thin to 6" apart when seedlings are established.

### *Lobelia cardinalis* (Cardinal flower)
Another splendid plant for boglike conditions or to enhance water gardens. Spires of brilliant red, blue, or white blossoms over a basal rosette of foliage. 2–3'. Thrives in full sun to semishade in moist, rich soil. Cannot survive drought conditions. This plant is quite lovely, but is difficult to grow. You may or may not have luck with it.

### *Lupinus* (Lupine)
Tall thick flower spikes of white, cream yellow, pink, red, blue, purple, orange, and combinations thereof over palm-shaped leaves that remain presentable throughout the season. 4–5'. Thrives in full sun or semishade in a deep moist acid loam. Fertilize with 5–10–5 each spring and summer. Cannot survive drought conditions. There are many native varieties available, including the Texas Bluebonnet. For traditional garden usage, select the Russell hybrids. Although lupines might be short lived in many areas, they are easily grown from seed. But remember, the seeds you plant in any given year will not bloom until the following year.

### *Lychnis coronaria* (Rose campion) 🐛
Cerise or white blossoms on silver-gray, woolly textured foliage. 24–36". Thrives in full sun. Plant outdoors in mid-spring or fall. Deadhead after bloom to encourage new flowers.

### *Lysimachia clethroides* (Gooseneck or Japanese loosestrife) 🐛
Weedy perennial with white blossoms resembling a gooseneck. Hairy leaves. 2–3'. A nice cutting flower. Do not plant in a border or bed but only where you need a plant that can and will take over and offer some bloom. If you do plant it in an orderly bed, you will live to regret it.

*Lysimachia punctata* (Yellow loosestrife) ❧
Yellow blooms on leafy, upright stems useful in places where nothing else seems to grow. 3'. Do not plant in a border or bed but use only in distant areas of the garden where law and order can be ignored: it's invasive.

*Lythrum salicaria* 'Morden's Pink' ❧ 🦌
Deep pink spires of blossoms on medium-green, willowlike foliage. 4–6'. Not fussy about soil. Thrives in full sun but will grow in partial shade. Plant in mid-spring or fall. In some areas, lythrum is illegal to plant because it is very invasive in boggy areas. However, in most areas, it is a nice addition to the perennial border, and named varieties–'Morden's Pink' is sterile–are easily contained.

*Malva moschata* (Musk mallow, marsh mallow) ❧
Five-petaled, flamboyant, pink, white or red blossoms. 24–36". Thrives in alkaline soil in full sun or partial shade. It resides profusely and can become a nuisance unless unwanted seedlings are removed. Deadhead after bloom to avoid problem.

*Mertensia* (Virginia bluebells)
Clusters of blue, bell-shaped blossoms over basal rosettes of wide green leaves. 1–2'. Thrives in semishade or full shade in average moist soil. Plant is completely dormant from late spring, after bloom, until the following spring. Foliage dries and plant remains inert. For this reason, summer drought is not a problem. Combines spectacularly with spring bulbs such as daffodils.

*Monarda* (Bee balm, bergamot, or Oswego tea) 🦌
Bright red, white, purple, or pink 3" whorls of feathery blossoms over medium-green foliage. 2–3'. Thrives in full sun or partial shade in moist soil. Plant outdoors in mid-spring or fall and deadhead after bloom. Leaves are very prone to mildew, so plant where air circulation is good. The leaves are used to make tea and are the ingredient that gives the Earl Grey tea blend its distinctive flavor.

*Oenothera tetragona* (Evening primrose) ❧ 🦌
Yellow or pink buttercuplike blossoms on elegant, medium-green foliage. 12–24". Thrives in well-drained, sandy soil in full sun. Plant in mid-spring. Spreads rapidly but can be contained.

*Paeonia* (Peony)
Single or double pompon blossoms in pink, coral, white, burgundy, yellow, and combinations thereof on lustrous, dark green foliage that remains attractive throughout the season. 24–48". Thrives in enriched soil in full sun. Needs moisture. Plant outdoors in August or early September. Deadhead after bloom. Cut foliage to ground after killing frost, as disease can be harbored in foliage over the winter.

*Papaver orientale* (Oriental poppy) ❧ 🦌
Large cup-shaped blossoms in white, scarlet, orange, pink, peach, and combinations thereof. 24–36". Thrives in full sun. Plant outdoors in early spring or fall. Remove foliage when it dries during midsummer. Plant goes dormant after flowering, so summer drought is rarely a problem. Overplant with annuals after bloom to cover the bare spot in the garden.

*Perovskia* (Russian sage) ❧
Powder blue spikes of tiny blossoms on delicate gray foliage. 2–3'. Thrives in enriched, well-drained soil in full sun. Plant outdoors in early spring. Cut back to 6" in early spring. Practically indestructible.

*Phlox paniculata* (Perennial phlox) ❧
White, pink, purple, red, lavender, or orange, often with contrasting eye. Large flower head composed of individual florets on stiff stalks with medium-green foliage. 4'. Thrives in enriched soil in full sun but tolerates partial shade. Plant outdoors in mid-spring or fall. Deadhead after bloom. Cut foliage to ground after killing frost. Phlox is subject to mildew, so plant in areas where air circulation is good.

*Physostegia virginiana* (Obedient plant) ✿
Pink or white snapdragon-shaped blossoms on tidy spear-shaped foliage. 2–5'. Thrives in full sun or partial shade. Drought resistant, although plants will be somewhat dwarfed in dry climates. Plant outdoors anytime during growing season. A late bloomer, at a time when many of the garden perennials are finished blooming.

*Platycodon* (Balloon flower)
Purple, white, or pink balloon-shaped blossoms in spikes over medium-green foliage, depending on variety. 12–30". Thrives in enriched soil in full sun but tolerates partial shade. Needs moisture. Plant outdoors in mid-spring or fall. Deadhead after bloom to encourage rebloom. Balloon flower is difficult to transplant because of its long taproot but can be propagated from seed. Very dependable once established.

*Polygonatum* (Solomon's seal)
Graceful cream bells on arching stems with thick oval foliage. 2–4', depending on variety. Thrives in deep, moist soil but will sustain drought and tree root competition once established. Prefers semishade or full shade. Full sun is not satisfactory. 'Variegatum' has green leaves tipped with white.

*Primula japonica* (Japanese primrose) ✿
Whorls of rose, purple, or white blossoms over bright-green foliage. 2'. Must have shade and moisture to succeed. Plant in the spring or fall. Particularly useful around water gardens and natural ponds.

*Pulmonaria angustifolia* (Blue lungwort) ✿
Deep blue, pink, or white flowers over spear-shaped clumps of green leaves blotched with silver. 9"–1'. Thrives in moist, rich soil in semishade or full shade. A very early-blooming perennial that is a fine companion to yellow daffodils at the beginning of the spring season. Foliage remains attractive all summer; often used as a ground cover for that reason.

*Rudbeckia* (Coneflower) ✿ ⚘
Gold, yellow, or rust-colored daisylike blossoms on medium-green foliage, depending on variety. 2–5'. Thrives in full sun. Plant outdoors in mid-spring or fall. Deadhead after bloom to encourage new flowers. *Rudbeckia hirta* is black-eyed Susan. Easy to grow, producing extravagant bloom.

*Salvia* (Sage) ✿ ✿
A large group of plants sporting white, pink, purple, blue, or red blossoms on deep-green and flamboyantly variegated foliage in green and pink, green and yellow, purple and gray, depending on variety. 3–5'. Thrives in moderately fertile, light sandy soil in full sun or partial shade. Plant outdoors in mid-spring or fall. Deadhead after bloom to encourage new flowers. Deep purple 'Victoria' and intense blue 'Sunny Border Blue' are particular favorites of mine.

*Saponaria officinalis* (Bouncing Bet) ✿
Pink or red clusters of double blossoms. 2–3". Thrives in well-drained soil in full sun. Sprawls all over in rich soil. Plant anytime during the growing season. If plants get leggy in the spring, trim back to encourage bushiness.

*Solidago odora* (Goldenrod) ✿ ⚘
Golden, plumelike blossoms on medium-green foliage. 2–3'. Thrives in well-drained soil in full sun or part shade. Plant in mid-spring or sow seeds in situ in early spring. Hybrids of our wild goldenrod are a permanent planting in a great many gardens in Europe. Take a fresh look at goldenrod. You may well decide to include it in your garden.

*Stokesia laevis* ✿
Pink, white, lavender, and lovely blue pincushionlike blossoms on clumps of spear-shaped, evergreen foliage. 1–2'. Thrives in moderately fertile sandy soil in full sun or partial shade. Wet feet will kill the plant. This is a marvelous plant, pest and disease free, tidy, requiring no special care. It blooms its head off all summer long.

*Thalicritum* (Meadow rue)

Cloudlike lavender, pink, or white clusters of blossoms, depending on variety, on medium-green, columbine-leaf foliage. 2–5'. Thrives in areas with ordinary soil as well as in swampy areas, in full sun or partial shade. *Thalicritum aquilegifolium* is the most popular variety, and it blooms in late spring in tandem with tulips.

*Verbascum* 'Southern Charm' ☙

The name says it all. This plant has it. Pink, rose, and white spires of 1" blossoms on sturdy, medium-green foliage. 3–4'. Not fussy about soil. Prefers full sun. Cut spent flower stalks back for a second bloom, which may or may not occur, depending on growing conditions.

*Veronica* (Speedwell) ❀ ☙

Blue, lavender, white, or pink spikes or clusters of blossoms on medium-green, lustrous foliage. 2–36". Thrives in well-drained, sandy soil in full sun but tolerates partial shade. Plant outdoors in early spring. Deadhead for repeat bloom.

*Yucca* ❀ ☙

Large bell-shaped, white or violet-tinged blossoms, over rosettes of green or variegated swordlike foliage. 4–6'. Thrives in well-drained, sandy, poor soil in full sun. For occasional dramatic accents and a tropical look, nothing beats yucca. But use it sparingly.

# Roses

The wonderful world of roses is far too large to be covered here. If it has always been your dream to have a breathtakingly beautiful country rose garden, then visit your local nursery or garden center and discuss your needs with them. They can advise you about which roses and/or classes of roses thrive in your area. But keep in mind that growing many roses, particularly "modern" roses, that is, the hybrid teas, requires a great deal of care and time. If you neglect

them, you will end up with an ugly patch of dead-looking sticks and disease-ridden leaves. I've always said that having thirty rose bushes or fruit trees is like having thirty beagles to look after. Each requires special attention and, in many cases, different treatment.

You can use roses as shrubs, hedges, or climbers, but almost all need at least six to seven hours of full sun a day. And these days more and more people are working rose bushes into informal perennial or shrub borders rather than planting them all together in a formal rose garden. Most require fortified soil and a reasonable amount of care, including watering, feeding, spraying, and pruning, in order to fulfill their potential. The three main classifications of roses are old garden roses (often called "old-fashioned roses"), modern roses, and shrub roses, and each group includes climbing varieties. Among roses, the shrubs tend to be larger and more sprawling than the stiffer modern bushes. Here are some of the types you might encounter in plant catalogues, with some recommendations.

## Old garden roses

These roses, such as the highly fragrant Cabbage, Damask, Gallica, and Alba roses, the pride of nineteenth-century horticulture, are now enjoying a renewed popularity with gardeners. Not only are they intensely fragrant, but their bloom is profuse, most are disease resistant, and some even drought resistant, making them a good selection for a weekend country garden. Be sure to look into this class of roses and make room for some on your property. You will not regret it. Unlike hybrids, most offer only one flush of bloom per season, in late spring, although Damasks sometimes bloom two or three times a season. Many grow into large, somewhat unruly plants, and they need space to be displayed to their best advantage.

## Modern roses

These are the familiar hybrid teas, the results of twentieth-century hybridization. They are, of course, lovely to look at, but they require a great deal of care, and unfortunately much of the heady rose fragrance has been bred out of the flower. You must water, prune, spray, feed, and keep the bed tidy. If you do not have time to fuss, and I mean lots of time, avoid this class of roses completely. Like fruit trees, they are work. For many years, my rose garden was my pride and joy. It was the first garden I installed twenty-five years ago when I bought my country house, evoking many happy memories of times and people long since gone. About ten years ago, I simply did not have time to fuss over it anymore. There were too many other gardens on the property that I was working on, limiting the time allocated to the rose garden, so I dug them all up and gave them away.

And then, the English roses were introduced. These are the magnificent new hybrids that are the culmination of nearly forty years of research and rose breeding by David Austin of Great Britain. They are the result of crossing old garden roses with modern bush roses. For form and flower, delicacy of coloring, and rich fragrance, they can be compared with Damask, Gallica, and Alba roses, and they bloom repeatedly throughout the season. Because they are far less demanding of ideal conditions than other modern roses, they are an excellent bet for a weekend country garden.

I have planted quite a few but have chosen to work them into existing shrub and perennial borders, as the British and Irish do, rather than in separate "rose beds." The old Floribundas, now called cluster-flowered roses, are also a good choice for country garden landscaping. Generally speaking, they are disease and drought resistant, tough old birds that are determined to reward you with a respectable, attractive bloom. 'Betty Prior' is a very popular pink cluster-flowered rose because it will grow almost anywhere and seems to thrive on neglect. Another is 'Ballerina,' a pink cluster rose with a white eye, also determined to bloom its head off. If you dead head the clusters, the rose will bloom on and on until a very deep freeze. 'The Fairy' is another cultivar that is nearly indestructible and requires little care other than pruning.

'New Dawn' climber

Rosa rugosa

'America' climber

'Blaze' climber

'Ballerina' shrub rose

English rose

### Shrub roses

There are both modern and wild shrub roses. They grow 3–5', depending on variety, with white, pink, red, yellow, or orange-toned blossoms. These are tough plants, and if they are happy, they become hedges, thick with profuse bloom. There are many modern varieties available and most are easy to grow, disease and drought resistant, a fine choice for the busy country gardener. They are a good selection for distant or difficult areas of your property, where, if left alone, they will provide stunning displays throughout the growing season. The wild varieties, *Rosa rugosa* (pink single flowers) and *R. rugosa alba* (white single flowers), will thrive in almost any environment without care. In the fall, after a summer of bloom, the plant rewards you with brilliant red rose hips, and the handsome green leathery foliage turns a bright orange in the fall.

### Climbing roses

If you have the space, include climbers in your planting scheme, as they offer extravagant bloom. The branches do not attach themselves to surfaces but must be tied to trellises, fences, and other supports. Be sure to take note of the ultimate height of climbing roses. Most are very vigorous and many can exceed their bounds in a very short time. I had 'New Dawn,' a delicate pink climbing rose, on a fence that was sixteen feet long. In two years it started to become predatory, it had completely outgrown the fence, and I was convinced that every time I passed it the love-starved thorny branches would reach out and try to embrace me. I finally dug it up and gave it away.

### Miniature roses

These are charming, lilliputian versions of the larger varieties growing to a mere 1', sporting tiny blossoms. They require a great deal of care and are more suited to the hobbyist rather than the busy weekend gardener.

# Shrubs

Most shrubs included are hardy to Zone 5, with many hardy to Zones 2 and 3. Some are hardy only to Zone 6 or Zone 7.

*Abelia* X *grandiflora* (Glossy abelia)
Deciduous shrub. Pinkish white flowers in the summer and fall on finely textured, glossy, deep-green arching foliage, which turns bronze in the fall. 4'. Thrives in well-drained soil, semishade to full sun, and average moisture. Hardy to Zone 6.

*Acer palmatum* var. *dissectum* (Looseleaf Japanese maple)
Deciduous shrub. A slow-growing, dwarf tree used as a shrub, sporting soft, wispy foliage. Many shades of red and green, some with variegated leaves. 6–8'. Thrives in well-drained acid soil rich in organic matter, in filtered shade with protection from heavy winds. Autumn foliage of many varieties is spectacular. Hardy to Zone 6.

*Berberis thunbergii* (Japanese barberry) 🦋 🐦 🦌
Deciduous shrub. Red berries in the fall and foliage of red, yellow, purple, dark green, or with variegations, depending on variety. 2–5'. Thrives in sandy soil. A compact, thorny shrub often used for hedges because it takes pruning well. The thorns tend to collect debris, which can be difficult to remove. Hardy to Zone 5.

*Buddleia davidii* (Butterfly bush, summer lilac) 🦋 🐦 🦌
Deciduous shrub. Showy lilaclike spikes of white, yellow, deep-blue, pink, red, or purple clusters of blossoms on medium-green foliage. 6–15', but can be controlled by pruning. Foliage dies down to the ground in the winter, growing again to mature height in the spring. Cut back to 4–6" in late fall or early spring before new growth commences. Attracts butterflies. Hardy to Zone 5.

*Buxus* (Box) 🦋 🦌
Broad-leaved evergreen shrub. The traditional shrub for

hedges, tightly branched, with small lustrous leaves. 3–6', depending on variety, of which there are many in cultivation. Thrives in sun or partial shade. Drought resistant once established. Not hardy north of Zone 6 and not used more widely because of its susceptibility to extreme cold. Dwarf forms are ideal for edging beds.

### *Callicarpa* (Beauty berry) ❀

Deciduous shrub. Grown for its unusual small clusters of bright purple berries in the fall, which are over medium-green foliage. 4–6'. Thrives in sun or partial shade. Drought resistant once established. A great addition to the autumn garden.

### *Calluna vulgaris* (Heather, Scotch heather)

Evergreen shrub. Small scalelike overlapping leaves and sprays of pretty little pale purple-to-pink flowers. 3'. There are many cultivars, in a range of colors and blooming period, from summer to early fall. Prefers sandy, acidic soil.

### *Camellia japonica*

Broad-leaved evergreen shrub. Glorious, large single and double blossoms in white, red, pink, and combinations thereof over dense, polished, dark evergreen foliage. 6–12'. Thrives in partial to deep shade depending on variety in soil that is fortified with organic matter and slightly acid. Blooms from early to late spring. *Camellia sasanqua* is similar to *C. japonica* but blooms in autumn and winter. Hardy to Zone 7B.

### *Caryopteris* X *clandonensis* (Bluebeard) ❀

Deciduous shrub. Spires of blue or purplish blue blossoms in late summer and fall on silvery green foliage. 3–4'. Cut back to 6" in late winter or early spring. If location is ideal, plant will self-sow. You can avoid seedlings by cutting all flowering stems after bloom, but you may find the plant so attractive and useful that you will want lots of them to transplant elsewhere in the garden. Hardy to Zone 5.

### *Chaenomeles speciosa* (Flowering quince) ❀

Deciduous shrub. Spectacular early spring blossoms in scar-let, apricot, white, pink, and coral on medium-green foliage. 6–10'. A tough plant that thrives in full sun or semishade. There are many new varieties available, but try to select those that are thornless, as debris collects in thorny cultivars. Hardy to Zone 5.

### *Chamaecyparis* (False cypress) ❀

Coniferous shrub. Globular, pyramidal, and spreading forms in silver, blue, green, or gold foliage, depending on variety. Hardy from Zones 4 to 8, depending on variety. Recommended dwarf varieties include:

*C. obtusa* 'Aurea Nana' (Dwarf gold Hinoki cypress): Heavy gold foliage.

*C. obtusa* 'Gracilis Anna': Deep-green foliage, upright growth habit.

*C. obtusa* 'Kosteri Nana': Lacy foliage, broad growth habit.

*C. obtusa* 'Tortulosa Anna' (Dwarf twisted branch cypress): Branches are twisted; compact, irregular, pyramidal form.

*C. pisifera* 'Argentea Anna' (Dwarf silver cypress): Soft plumed silvery blue foliage; dense globular growth habit. 'Argentea Variegata Anna' has variegated foliage.

*C. pisifera* 'Aurea Pendula' (Dwarf gold thread cypress): Bright golden pendulous filaments; dense, low-growing shrub. Does not burn in sun.

*C. pisifera* 'Minima' (Dwarf threadleaf cypress): Green foliage; compact growth habit.

*C. pisifera* 'Sulfuria Anna' (Dwarf sulfur cypress): Bright sulfur-colored foliage; broad growth habit.

*C. pisifera* var. *filifera* 'Aurea Variegata Anna' (Dwarf gold variegated cypress): Gold variegated foliage.

### *Clethra alnifolia* (Sweet pepperbush, summer-sweet) ❀

Deciduous native shrub. Spikes of white or pink flower in late summer followed by black seeds that look like peppercorns on medium-green foliage. 4–6'. Thrives in wet or dry sandy soil and in sun or partial shade. Hardy to Zone 3.

**Cornus sericea** (Red osier dogwood) 🦌
Deciduous native shrub. Small white blossoms in late spring and white berries in the summer on medium-green foliage. To 7'. The red bark is particularly lovely in the snow. Regretfully, this cultivar is beginning to succumb to the anthracnose disease that affects it's regal cousin, *Cornus florida*. C. 'Flaviramea' (golden-twig dogwood) sports yellow stems. Hardy to Zone 2.

**Cotinus coggygria** (Smokebush) ❀
Deciduous shrub. Cloudlike pink or white blossoms on spectacular purple foliage. 6–25', depending on variety. For the most intense purple foliage, select 'Velvet Cloak.' Thrives in dry, rocky soil and full sun. Once established, it is drought resistant. To keep size under control, cut back to about 1' in late winter or very early spring. Hardy to Zone 4.

**Cotoneaster** (Cotoneaster) ❀ 🌱
Broad-leaved evergreen shrub. A wide range of cultivars either upright or creeping, most with white or pink blossoms in the spring and red berries in the fall on lustrous, deep-green foliage. 2–20", depending on variety. Drought resistant once established. Cotoneaster is especially useful to cover a sunny bank or to control erosion. Hardy to from Zones 5 to 9, depending on variety. Varieties that are tough and fast growing include:

C. *dammeri* (Bearberry cotoneaster): Low-growing (18") and useful as a ground cover, although technically a shrub.

C. *divaricatus* (Spreading cotoneaster): A carefree shrub that sports brilliant yellow and red long-lasting foliage in the fall, to 6'.

C. *horizontalis* (Rockspray cotoneaster): Another lower growing variety (24–36") that makes a beautiful fall display.

C. *multiflorus* (Many-flowered cotoneaster): A tall-growing variety (8–12') sporting fragrant white blossoms in May and brilliant red berries from August to October.

**Cytisus scoparius** (Scotch broom) ❀
Deciduous or semievergreen shrub. Yellow, crimson, apricot, lilac, and tricolored pealike blossoms on upright shrub with needlelike foliage. To 6'. Thrives in full sun. In the landscape, the small, inconspicuous foliage offers a nice contrast to the more lush foliage of other shrubs. Hardy to Zone 6.

**Daphne X burkwoodii** (Burkwood daphne) ❀
Broad-leaved evergreen shrub. Rosy-pink or white clusters of fragrant blossoms on evergreen glossy foliage, some variegated. 3–4'. Thrives in full sun or semishade. Drought resistant once established. Very easy to grow. 'Carol Mackie' is a recommended variety. Hardy to Zone 5.

**Deutzia gracilis** (Slender deutzia) ❀
Deciduous shrub. Rosy-pink to white clusters of blossoms on dark-green foliage. 2–6', depending on variety. Thrives in full sun or semishade. Drought resistant once established. Prune immediately after flowering, as it flowers on old wood. Very easy to grow; an old-fashioned favorite. Hardy to Zone 5.

**Euonymus alata** (Burning-bush, winged euonymus) ❀
Deciduous shrub. Grown for its spectacular cherry-red fall foliage. Thrives in full sun or heavy shade. 4–20', depending on variety. Drought resistant once established. Locate the plant where it can grow to its full height for pruning creates unattractive broomlike growth. 'Rudy Haag' and 'Anna' grow 4–6', manageable for the average garden. Hardy to Zone 4.

**Forsythia** ❀ 🦌
Deciduous shrub. Yellow or cream-colored blossoms in early spring on upright or weeping shrub with bright-green foliage. 6–8'. Avoid weeping versions as they require annual pruning to keep them under control once established. Drought resistant once established. Upright varieties such as *Forsythia* X *intermedia* 'Linwood Gold' are recommended. Prune after flowering rather than in the fall or early spring for most profuse display each season. Hardy to Zone 5.

Scotch broom

*Below*: Tree peony

Buddleia

*Left*: Spirea

*Fothergilla major* (Fothergilla) ❀
Deciduous shrub. Honey-scented white blossoms on dark-green, pest-free foliage that provides a colorful fall display of red, orange, yellow, and scarlet. 6–10'. Adaptable but prefers acid, well-drained soil in full sun or partial shade. Drought resistant once established. Dwarf variety is *Fothergilla gardenii*. 6–8'. Hardy to Zone 6.

*Hamamelis* X *Intermedia* (Hybrid witchhazel)
Deciduous shrub. Spice-scented, bright-yellow flowers on twiggy, somewhat ungainly plant. 15–20', although can be kept dwarf and manageable by judicious pruning. Thrives in deep rich soil with considerable moisture. Plant in full sun or light shade. Grown primarily for the very early yellow blossoms, which offer a lift to the spirits during the doldrums of late February and early March. Hardy to Zone 6.

*Hebe*
Broad-leaved evergreen shrub. White or pink blossoms on leathery foliage. Like pachysandra, Hebe can be easily propagated from cuttings. *Hebe* X *andersonii*, a white, late-summer-blooming species, to 4', and 'Variegata,' with leaves edged in cream, are widely available. *H. decumbens* (ground hebe), with small gray leaves edged in red and small spikes of white blossoms in the spring, also is recommended. Hardy to Zone 6.

*Hibiscus syriacus* (Rose of Sharon, althaea) ❀
Deciduous shrub or small tree. An old-fashioned favorite, cultivated in North America for more than two hundred years. White, white and burgundy, rose, or blue blossoms, resembling the southern hibiscus, on medium-green foliage. To 15'. Nearly indestructible, but beware of older varieties that self-seed everywhere. The only nonself-seeding variety is the recently introduced 'Diane,' a pure white, which is utterly breathtaking and blooms its head off from the end of June until frost. Hardy to Zone 5.

*Hydrangea macrophylla* (French hydrangea)
Deciduous shrub. Large blue, white, or pink pompon-shaped

blossoms in mid- to late summer on handsome deep-green foliage. 3–6'. Tolerates shade. Roots prefer moist conditions, so be sure to provide sufficient water during summer drought. Plant will tell you if it needs watering by wilting visibly. If you prefer blue bloom, try scratching one tablespoon of an acid fertilizer such as Miracid into the ground around the plant when shoots first emerge in the spring. For pink bloom, substitute one tablespoon of garden lime. Hardy to Zone 7.

*Hydrangea quercifolia* (Oakleaf hydrangea)
Deciduous shrub. Lacy white flower clusters on coarse, deep-green foliage. 6–8', but can be pruned to maintain dwarf size. Thrives in moist, slightly acid, fertile, well-drained soil in full sun or semishade. Will tolerate deep shade. Flowers on old wood, so prune after summer bloom. Hardy to Zone 6.

*Hypericum prolificum* (Shrubby St.-John's-wort) ❀
Deciduous shrub. Bright yellow blossoms on handsome blue-green foliage. 1–4'. Grows in any soil in full sun or semishade. Easy to grow, with blossoms that persist from June until fall. You get your money's worth with this one. Hardy to Zone 5.

*Juniperus* (Juniper) ❀
Coniferous shrub. Creeping, low and spreading, vase-shaped and columnar, with varying shades of green, blue, or gold foliage. Hardy from Zones 4 to 10, depending on variety. Recommended varieties are:
   *J. chinensis* 'Blue Vase' (Blue vase juniper): Vase-shaped growth habit, to 5'.
   *J. chinensis* 'Japonica' (Japanese juniper): Semi-upright in habit; deeply textured foliage in slate to green shades.
   *J. chinensis* 'Old Gold' (Old gold juniper): Golden yellow in color.
   *J. chinensis* 'Pfitzerana Aura' (Gold tip juniper): Bright golden color in the spring and summer.
   *J. chinensis* 'Torulosa' (Hollywood juniper): Dense shrub with twisted branches, to 6'.

*J. chinensis* var. *procumbens* 'Anna' (Dwarf Japanese juniper, Pronina juniper): Short stiff branches forming a carpet up t 6' across, mounting to 10" in the center.

*J. horizontalis* 'Bar Harbor' (Bar Harbor juniper): Creeping form; steel blue foliage with a fernlike appearance.

*J. horizontalis* 'Blue Chip' ( Blue chip juniper): Silvery blue foliage, spreading, low-mounding habit.

*J. horizontalis* 'Glauca' (Blue creeping juniper): Creeping form, blue foliage.

*J. horizontalis* 'Plumosa' (Andorra juniper): Low-spreading habit, summer foliage silvery green turning purple after frost.

*J. rigida* 'Pendula' (Weeping needle juniper): Narrow, tall, and pendant in habit.

### *Kalmia latifolia* (Mountain laurel) 🦌

Broad-leaved evergreen. Large clusters of white to deep pink blossoms over elegant evergreen foliage. 3–15', depending on variety. Thrives in acid, cool, moist, well-drained soil in full sun to partial shade. Traditionally used as a companion planting to azaleas and rhododendrons. Hardy to Zone 5.

### *Kerria japonica* (Japanese rose) ❁

Deciduous shrub. Single or double, bright yellow, powderpuff blossoms on green foliage. 3–6'. A tough plant that thrives in poor soil and in partial shade. Prune after bloom as it flowers on last year's wood. A good selection for areas with little sun and for surface root areas under maple and beech trees. Hardy to Zone 5.

### *Kolkwitzia amabilis* (Beauty bush) ❁ 🦌

Deciduous shrub. My own feeling is that beauty bush is overused in North America, but this 10', medium-green foliage shrub can be used as a windbreak. Most specimens sport washed-out pink blossoms, but look for deeper pink blooming plants at local nurseries, often called 'Rosea.' Seed clusters follow the blossoms, and the brown bark falls from stems in long strips. Autumn foliage is red. Hardy to Zone 5.

### *Lagerstroemia indica* (Crape myrtle)

Deciduous shrub. Showy clusters of plum, white, pink, and crimson blossoms in midsummer on bronze foliage, maturing to green that turns to orange, yellow, and scarlet in the fall. 5–25', depending on variety. Thrives in well-drained moist soil in a hot, sunny location. For most country gardens, select from the dwarf varieties that grow 5–10'. Hardy to Zone 7B.

### *Leucothoe fontanesiana* (Drooping leucothoe) 🦌

Broad-leafed evergreen shrub. Delicate white blossoms in early spring on handsome bright-green or bronze glossy foliage. 3–6'. Thrives in moist, well-drained acid soil in full sun or full shade. Traditionally, a companion plant to rhododendrons, azaleas, and mountain laurel. Hardy to Zone 5.

### *Ligustrum* (Privet) ❁ 🕊

Deciduous or semievergreen shrub. Privet bears white flower clusters in the spring but is grown primarily for its glossy foliage. To 15'. The ubiquitous hedging plant used for windbreaks and privacy screening. There are numerous varieties to choose from, especially *Ligustrum ovalifolium* (California privet) and *L. vulgaris* (common privet). For a very special effect high prune plants so that the silvery bark of their stems is revealed. Hardy from Zones 4 to 10, depending on variety.

### *Magnolia stellata* (Star magnolia)

Deciduous shrub. Large white star-shaped blossoms in early spring. 6–20', depending on variety. Thrives in deep, rich, well-drained, moist soil in full sun to partial shade. Select from dwarf varieties that are more in scale with the average country garden. Hardy to Zone 5.

### *Nandina domestica* (Heavenly bamboo) ❁

Deciduous shrub. Creamy white blossom spikes on delicate, deep-green, evergreen foliage. 4–6'. By fall, clusters of bright red berries cover the plant. Thrives in almost any kind of soil in sun or shade. Drought resistant when established. If plant dies to the ground in the winter, it will send up new shoots in the spring. Hardy to Zone 6 with protection.

*Paeonia suffruticosa* (Tree peony)
Deciduous shrub. Spectacular, enormous red, white, pink, yellow, orange, and purple single and double blossoms on attractive large leaves. 3–4'. Thrives in well-drained soil that has been enriched with organic material in full sun or partial shade. Long-lasting plants that become more and more beautiful with each passing year. Do not confuse these with herbaceous peonies, which you cut back to the ground every fall. Leave the plant alone since all leaves and blossoms will emerge from established wood. Hardy to Zone 5.

*Philadelphus coronarius* (Sweet mock orange) ❀
Deciduous shrub. Highly fragrant, white blossoms on leggy stems and coarse foliage. This tough plant, free from pests, adapts to any soil and thrives in full sun or partial shade. 10–12'. Prune after flowering by removing older wood or cut to ground. Beyond its fragrant flowers, which bloom for only two weeks, the plant has little to offer. Hardy to Zone 5.

*Picea abies* 'Nidiformis' (Bird's-nest spruce) ❧
Coniferous shrub. This dwarf spruce with delicate needles forms a dense, low mound. 3–6'. Thrives in well-drained, sandy soil. Thrives in full sun or partial shade. A fine selection for rock gardens, mountainous areas with rock outcroppings, or foundation plantings. Hardy to Zone 2.

*Picea albertiana glauca* 'Conica' (Alberta spruce) ❀ ❧
Coniferous shrub. This dwarf slow-growing conical spruce grows only 1–2" a year, ultimately reaching 6–8'. Thrives in many different soil types in full sun or partial shade. Like its cousin above, Alberta spruce adapts well to rock gardens and to rocky mountainous areas. It is a useful plant for the gardener. Hardy to Zone 2.

*Pieris japonica* (Andromeda) ❧
Broad-leaved evergreen shrub. Small clusters of white blossoms in the spring on lustrous 3"–long leaves. 6'. Andromeda is one of the earliest of the broad-leafed evergreens to bloom and therefore is useful in combination with early spring-blooming bulbs such as daffodils and hyacinths. Thrives in partial shade and moist, acid soil. Hardy to Zone 6.

*Potentilla fruticosa* (Bush cinquefoil) ❀
Deciduous native shrub. Small yellow, white, orange, or burgundy blossoms through summer and into fall on foliage that resembles strawberry leaves. To 4'. Will not bloom unless grown in full sun. Survives in poor, dry soil with little moisture, but, of course, will grow better in enriched soil and with regular watering. There are many named varieties available: 'Bee,' 'Katherine Dikes,' and 'Vilmoriniana' are a few. Hardy to Zone 2.

*Pyracantha coccinea* (Scarlet firethorn) ❀ ❦
Broad-leaved evergreen shrub. Clusters of white flowers over evergreen or semievergreen foliage. 6–18'. Grown primarily for stunning red or orange berries in the fall. Thrives in well-drained soil in full sun. Control growth by judicious annual pruning. A spectacular addition to the fall garden. Most cultivars hardy to Zone 7.

*Rhododendron* (Rhododendrons and azaleas)
Broad-leaved evergreen shrub. Thousands of varieties, with flamboyant clusters of blossoms in the complete color spectrum in the spring on lustrous dark or medium-green evergreen foliage. 6"–50' (but most are 2–8'), depending on variety. These shallow-rooted shrubs, which prefer moist, well-drained soil and tolerate partial shade, are ubiquitous in American gardens. In my opinion, it is best to buy rhododendrons and azaleas at local nurseries since they offer only those that are hardy in your area. Hardy to Zone 2–10, depending on variety.

*Spiraea* (wreath)
Deciduous shrub. Graceful, arching branches completely covered with white, pink, or red blossoms in late spring on medium-green foliage. To 6', depending on variety. Needs

sun and is not drought tolerant. Prune in the fall every few years to maintain vigor (remove branches at soil level). Fountain-shaped *Spiraea* X *Vanhouttei* is the most commonly planted variety. Hardy to Zone 5.

### *Syringa* (Lilac) 🌸 🦌

Deciduous shrub or small tree, Pink, white, lilac, blue, or deep-purple clusters of florets in late spring on medium-green foliage. Thrives in full sun. *Syringa vulgaris* (common lilac) is too tall (it grows to 20') for borders, but can be used for screens or planted in a grove in the distance. Lilacs that grow to a more manageable height are *Syringa* X *persica* (Persian lilac), with deep purple blooms (6'), and *S. oblata dilatata* (Korean early lilac), with pink blooms (5–6'). Deadhead flowers after bloom for a more profuse bloom the following year. Hardy to Zone 3B.

### *Taxus* (Yew) 🌸

Coniferous shrub. Medium- to deep-green needles on columnar, moundlike, and globular plants. Hardy from Zones 5 to 6B, depending on variety. The following varieties are recommended for country gardens:

*T. cuspidata* 'Densiformis' (Spreading Japanese yew): A mound-shaped shrub, spreading to 6', with medium-green needles that can be sheared to make hedges.

*T. fairview* (Fairview yew): Globular and compact in growth habit.

*T. aurea* 'Anna' (Golden dwarf yew): A dwarf with bright yellow-green foliage.

### *Thuja condensis* 'Pendulum' (Sergeant's weeping hemlock) 🌸

Coniferous shrub. One of the most attractive dwarf shrubs available. Growth habit is pendulous or weeping, with delicate evergreen needles. 5–6' at maturity, with a 8–9' spread. Thrives in well-drained acid soil in partial shade. Avoid windy areas or waterlogged soils and areas with summer temperatures more than 95 degrees. Make room for at least one of these very elegant shrubs on your property. Hardy to Zone 4.

### *Thuja occidentalis* (American arborvitae) 🌸

Coniferous native shrub. Pyramidal, conical, globular, and columnar forms with gold and light- to dark-green foliage. Hardy to Zone 2. Two useful varieties are 'Hetz's Midget' (dwarf globe arborvitae), a slow-growing, globular shrub with medium-green foliage, and *Thuja occidentalis woodwardii* (Woodward globe arborvitae), a bushy shrub that can even be used in window boxes.

### *Viburnum* 🌲

Deciduous shrub. Viburnums prefer sun. Hardy from Zones 5 to 10, depending on variety. Recommended varieties include:

*V.* X *burkwoodii* (Burkwood viburnum): Pink to white fragrant blossoms on upright habit with spear-shaped leaves, to 10'.

*V.* X *carlcephalum* (Snowball viburnum): Fragrant, snowball-shaped, white blossoms on lush green foliage, 6–10'.

*V. carlessi*: (Korean spice viburnum): Waxy, fragrant blossoms tinged pink in early spring on gray-green foliage that turns bronze-red in the fall, to 6'; shapely growth habit.

*V. dentatum* (Arrowhead): A native that adapts to boggy conditions, with attractive clusters of white blossoms in the spring followed by blue berries on deep-green foliage that turns bright red in autumn. 8–14'.

*V. plicatum* var. *tomentosum* (Doublefile virburnum): Lacy pure-white pinwheel blossoms on dark-green foliage with autumn color. Bright red fruits in midsummer. 8–10'. Many consider this the finest of all viburnums.

### *Vitex agnus-castus* (Chaste tree, hemp tree)

Deciduous shrub. Spectacular purple-blue spikes of flowers bloom in late summer and often again in mid-fall. Small leaves that are dark green on top and gray beneath. 10'. Thrives in areas of hot summers in full sun. New varieties thrive as far north as Zone 7a. Often multitrunked and shrubby in growth habit; for most pleasing result high prune to one trunk.

## Weigela ✿

Deciduous shrub. Scarlet, trumpet-shaped blossoms in late spring–early summer on medium-green foliage. 5–6'. Prefers partial shade where summers are hot. Weigela requires little care, but after a few years, old flowering wood should be pruned at soil level after the shrub blooms. Hardy to Zone 5.

# Trees

Almost all trees are drought resistant once established. Generally speaking, the mature height of trees can vary widely, depending entirely on growing conditions.

EVERGREEN TREES

### Abies concolor (White Colorado fir)

Pyramid form. Blue-green, 2" needles. To 120'. Prefers full sun. Of all the evergreens, this is perhaps the most heat resistant. Among the best selections are 'Violacea,' with bluish-white needles, and 'Conica,' which is a slow-growing dwarf variety.

### Cedrus deodora (Deodar cedar)

Pyramid form. Elegant tree with weeping branches. To 150'. 'Pendula' has branches that often touch the ground; 'Glauca' has blue-green or silvery-gray needles. Prefers full sun.

### Cedrus libani (Cedar of Lebanon)

Spreading form. One of the true aristocrats of the tree world. Slow-growing, needled, bright-green foliage. 40–70'. Large thick trunk and wide spread branches.

### Chamaecyparis (False cypress)

Conical or columnar forms. A very large group of evergreen trees with very small, scalelike leaves, in various shades of green, blue-green, and silver, many with variegated coloring of yellow, white, or silver. Most thrive in full sun and tolerate drought conditions. Consult locally for recommended cultivars.

### Cryptomeria japonica (Japanese cedar)

Conical form. Elegant evergreen with small, short needles. 6–150', depending on variety. Bark shreds creating trunk interest. Consult locally for recommended cultivars.

### Ilex (Holly) ✝ 🦌

A large group of useful trees and shrubs suitable for country environments. Hollies generally need sun to fruit out successfully, as well as a well-drained light soil They are dioecious, which means that there needs to be a male within about one-half mile of a female if you want fruiting trees. Both sexes bear flowers but only the female bears berries. Recommended varieties include:

I. cornuta (Chinese holly): Large, dark, shiny green leaves and red fruit. Compact form. 'Dwarf Burford' can be sheared into a dense, formal hedge. Drought tolerant but hardy only to Zone 7. Female plants set fruit without a male plant.

I. crenata (Japanese holly): Fine, glossy leaves and small black fruit. Various forms, most adaptable to shearing for hedges. Needs protection in Zone 6.

I. glabra (Inkberry): Inconspicuous black berries in late summer and fall on deep-green, shiny, oval leaves. Male and female plants are necessary for fruiting. Prefers a moist soil. Responds well to pruning.

I. opaca (American holly): The hardiest holly. Dark-green leaves and small red or orange fruit. Conical or open form, to 50'. Many varieties available.

I. pedunculosa (Longstalk holly): Glossy, oval leaves and red fruit on 1½" stalks. Similar in habit to American holly.

I. verticillata (Winterberry): Native deciduous shrub with many available garden varieties sporting different leaves and berries, ranging from red to orange to yellow. 4–15', depending on variety. Plant red-fruiting cultivars to attract birds. Winterberry grows best in full sun in very moist soil, but drought-resistant varieties are available.

I. X Meservae (Blue holly): Spiny blue-green leaves and red fruit. Rounded, compact form, 5–8'. Can be used for low, informal hedges. Hardy to Zone 6.

Witchhazel

Franklinia

Kousa dogwood

*Juniperus virginiana* (Eastern red cedar) ☂
Native, tough, and planted everywhere. Conical or columnar form. Slow-growing tree with small, scalelike leaves and blue cones that resemble berries. Can grow to 100' but rarely exceeds 40'. Thrives in full sun in ordinary to poor soil. Drought resistant once established. Can be used as a screen or hedge. Many varieties available.

*Picea* (Spruce) ☘
A large group of trees with short blue or green needles in mounded, conical, pendulous, and columnar forms. Thrives in full sun or partial shade. Drought resistant once established. Recommended varieties:

*P. mariana* 'Nana' (Dwarf black spruce): Mound-shaped with short, light gray-green needles.

*P. pungens* 'Glauca' (Dwarf Colorado or blue spruce): Conical dwarf with blue needles.

*P. pungens* 'Globosa' (Dwarf globe Colorado or blue spruce): Globe-shaped tree with silvery blue needles.

*Pinus* (Pine) ☂ 🦌
A large group of trees with long needles in shades of green and blue-green in mounded, columnar, pendulous, and conical shapes. Thrives in full sun or partial shade and resists drought once established. Recommended dwarf varieties include:

*P. mugo* (Mugo pine): Low-growing (and slow-growing) moundlike pine with long, bright-green needles. Very hardy.

*P. pumila* (Dwarf Siberian stone pine): Spreading habit with light blue-green to blue needles.

*P. strobus* 'Nana' (Dwarf white pine): Bushy habit with feathery blue-green needles.

*P. strobus* 'Ontario' (Dwarf Ontario white pine): Spreading habit with feathery blue-green needles.

*P. sylvestris* 'Watererii' (Dwarf Scotch pine): Compact, slow-growing form of Scotch pine. Conical when young and becoming rounded with age.

Recommended taller varieties include:

*P. sylvestris* (Scotch black pine): Compact, bushy tree. Very hardy.

Do not plant *P. thurnbergiana* (Japanese black pine) as it is being killed by a disease everywhere.

DECIDUOUS TREES

*Acer griseum* (Paperbark maple)
Dark-green foliage casts light shade and develops good fall color. Bark is an especially attractive cinnamon brown and strips from trunk naturally throughout growing season. Roundish shape to 25'. Prefers sun or partial shade and is moderately drought resistant once established. All maples have surface roots that absorb most of the moisture from the surrounding soil. Underplant only with shade-loving, drought-resistant ground covers or install pebbles or wood chips to retain moisture.

*Acer platanoides* (Norway maple)
An attractive shade tree, roundish in shape and densely branched with dark-green, leathery leaves. To 80'. Prefers sun or partial shade. Autumn foliage is brilliant yellow or orange-red. Norway maple has brittle branches that tend to split and break during heavy windstorms. Seedpods create a mess in the fall, and sprout up everywhere the following spring and summer. Many consider this a junk tree. Consult locally for recommended cultivars.

*Acer pseudoplatanus* (Sycamore maple)
Five-lobed leaves in various colors, depending on variety. To 90'. Prefers sun or partial shade. There is no colorful autumn foliage display. Consult locally for recommended cultivars.

*Betula pendula* (European white birch) ☂ ☘
Pyramidal weeping tree with white bark and small, glossy dark-green leaves. To 60'. Prefers full sun and normal soil. Tree has brittle branches, making it susceptible to damage in heavy windstorms, is subject to bronze birch borer infestation, and is short-lived, but its white bark is irresistible. The

native white birch, *B. populifolia*, is a small tree that often has multiple trunks. Consult locally for recommended cultivars.

### Cercis canadensis (Redbud)

Early, spring-flowering native offering a profusion of small, purple-pink blossoms that are followed by dried pods later. Heart-shaped leaves turn a brilliant yellow in the fall. 25'. Prefers full sun. *C. canadensis* var. *alba* sports white blossoms.

### Cornus florida (Flowering dogwood)

A tree of all seasons. Pink, white, or red blossoms cover the tree in the spring, handsome green foliage provides shade during summer, and brilliant red berries cover the tree in the fall. Foliage turns a rich red and crimson before leaves drop. Tree shape is from pyramidal to umbrella and wide-spreading, layered branches. To 30'. 'Cherokee Chief' is the new deep-pink flowering version. 'Cloud Nine' is a new very profuse white blooming cultivar. Unfortunately, many dogwoods throughout the country have been killed by fungal wilt disease and anthracnose. However, new hybrids that resist disease are being introduced each year, and the disease appears to be disappearing in some areas.

### Cornus kousa (Kousa dogwood, Japanese dogwood)

A good substitute if flowering dogwoods are threatened by disease in your area. Creamy white or whitish pink blossoms cover the tree in late spring and early summer, followed by pale red raspberrylike fruits, which are favored by the birds and which, in fact, are edible. Foliage is handsome, turning deep burgundy in the fall.

### Crataegus (Hawthorn)

This small tree bears either white or pinkish-red blossoms in the spring and red fruit in the summer. Leaves are a glossy dark-green and autumn foliage is brilliant red. Prefers full sun. *Crataegus crus-galli* (cockspur) and *C. phaenopyrum* (Washington hawthorn), both natives, are the two best cultivars for all environments, growing to 25'. Because their branches are thick with razor-sharp thorns, hawthorns are not a good tree to plant where children play. An unarmed variety of cockspur is available.

### Elaeagnus angustifolia (Russian olive)

Spreading, shrublike tree distinguished by its elegant, silvery foliage. Yellowish flowers in early spring are followed by silver berries in the fall. 12'. Thrives in full sun in any kind of soil. Grows fast and likes an occasional pruning. Birds are attracted by berries. *Elaeagnus umbellata* (autumn olive) is similar.

### Fagus sylvatica (European beech)

Probably the most aristocratic of all trees, it is prized for it's smooth gray bark; glossy, dark-green, copper, or purple foliage, depending on variety; and pendulous branching habit. The tree grows to 90' by 50–60' wide and is best grown on very large properties, parks, and golf courses so be sure you have a lot of space to show it off properly. Thrives in full sun.

### Franklinia alatamaha (Franklin tree)

Upright, pyramidal form. Lovely white camellialike flowers cover the tree from early August to November. Foliage is glossy green, turning brilliant orange-red in the fall. 20–25'. If tree is not happy, it will tell you so by dying. But it's worth a try because it is utterly breathtaking.

### Fraxinus (Ash)

A fast-growing native shade tree with handsome compound foliage. 50–80'. Prefers full sun. Select either *Fraxinus americana* (white ash), spectacular in yellow and purple in the fall, or the tougher *F. pennsylvanica* (green ash), with darker leaves and a more modest fall display

### Gleditsia triacanthose var. inermis (Thornless common honey locust)

Delicate bright-green foliage and fragrant pendulous clusters of white blossoms in late spring. 30–70'. Autumn foliage is yellow. Branches tend to snap during heavy wind or ice storms. Be sure to look for varieties that are seedless to avoid the mess of seedpod litter on the ground in late summer.

*Laburnum watereri* 'Vossii' (Golden-chain tree)
Grown for its spectacular 18" clusters of deep yellow, pea-shaped flowers. 20–30'. When grown as a tree, it is quite ordinary except for the two-week blooming period. But by pruning and training trees to a pergola, you can create a spectacular laburnum walk. When in bloom, the brilliant yellow panicles hang from the canopy structure. It is dazzling.

*Magnolia grandiflora* (Southern magnolia)
Much hardier than generally acknowledged. Specimens bloom in the Brooklyn Botanical Garden, as well as in Boston. Enormous, fragrant, creamy white flowers to 8" on glossy, heavy-textured, large leaves, make this one of the most beautiful trees on earth. 15–75', depending on variety. Dwarfs of manageable size for average-sized properties include 'St. Mary's' and 'Little Gem,' both readily available.

*Magnolia soulangiana* (Saucer magnolia)
Spectacular tree with large medium-green foliage, bearing pink, white, reddish purple, and, only recently, creamy or bright yellow blossoms in early spring. 20–30'. The new yellow 'Elizabeth' is simply gorgeous. Do not plant in a warm, sunny spot because blossoms will be forced to bloom and can be damaged by late frosts.

*Malus* (Flowering crab apple) ⫟
Beautiful small tree bearing white, pink, or deep-red blossoms in the spring. Many varieties offer small edible red crab apples in the summer and fall (technically, crab apples are apples under 2" in diameter). To 25'. Prefers full sun and moist soil. Dwarf and semidwarf varieties are available for use on patios and for small gardens. Standard-sized trees can be used as specimens, in borders, or as backdrops. It is a good idea to check at a reliable local nursery for the names of varieties recommended for your particular area.

*Nyassa sylvatica* (Pepperidge, sour gum, black gum, or black tupelo)
An East Coast native whose many common names testify to its wide appeal. Handsome leathery dark-green leaves turn brilliant orange to scarlet in the fall. 30–50'. Thrives in full sun or partial shade and in ordinary to moist soil. Drought resistant and also adapts to swampy conditions. Purchase only small specimens since taproot damage can kill tree.

*Prunus cerasifera* (Flowering plum)
Small flowering tree with white flowers in early spring followed by edible, plumlike fruit and glossy leaves. To 25'. Prefers full sun. Look for varieties with purple leaves, such as 'Nigra,' 'Rosea,' or 'Thundercloud.'

*Prunus serrulata* (Japanese flowering cherry) ⫟
White, pale, or deep-pink blossoms in the spring. More than a hundred varieties of this familiar and popular tree are available. 20–25'. Consult locally for recommended varieties.

*Quercus alba* (White oak) ⫟
The sturdy, familiar native tree. Dark-green, lobed leaves turn purplish red in autumn. To 90'. Slow-growing. Prefers full sun.

*Quercus palustris* (Pin oak)
Dense native of swampy woodlands. Graceful drooping branches with glossy jagged leaves that turn brilliant red in the fall. To 75'. Thrives in full sun.

*Robinia pseudoacacia* (Black locust)
Native, with light-green oval leaves, bearing pendulous clusters of fragrant white blossoms in late spring. To 75'. Prefers full sun. Consult with local nurseries regarding new disease-resistant varieties.

*Salix Matsudana* 'Tortuosa' (corkscrew willow, dragon-claw willow) ⫟
An interesting specimen tree with twisted shoots and leaves. To 20'. It is not fussy about soil. Although spectacularly beautiful, particularly beside a pond, be advised that the first trees to come down during a hurricane, tornado, or severe wind-

storm are the lovely weeping willows (*S. babylonica*) and the golden willow (*S. alba vitellina*). I don't recommend them.

***Styrax japonica*** (Japanese snowbell, Japanese snowdrop tree)
One of the choicest of small flowering trees, with clean foliage and tidy growth habit. Pendulous flowers similar to white fuchsia blossoms bloom for about a month in June. 15–20'. Thrives in rich well-drained soil. Prune to control shrub-like growth habit.

# Vines

All cultivars included are hardy to Zone 5, with many hardy to Zones 3 and 4. Annual vines, of course, are not hardy and are killed by the early frosts.

***Campsis radicans*** (Trumpet vine) 🐝
Perennial. Scarlet, orange, or yellow trumpetlike blossoms on vigorous vines with medium-green foliage. Grows to 50'. Thrives in full sun or partial shade. Plant outdoors in mid-spring or fall. Attracts hummingbirds. Do not plant on or near the facade of a house or outbuilding as vines grow through any openings. I have one in the wrong place on my property that I have been trying to kill for twenty years, and yet every year it sports new shoots and grows. A tough plant that is ideal for difficult growing conditions.

***Clematis*** 🦌
Perennial. Saucerlike blossoms in white, pink, red, blue, yellow, lavender, purple, and combinations thereof. 1–9" in diameter, depending on variety, on vines sporting handsome medium-green, glossy foliage. The flowers are followed by silvery seedpods. Thrives in moderately fertile, slightly alkaline soil in full sun or partial shade (the base of the plant should be shaded to keep roots cool). Requires moisture during summer drought. Plant in early to late spring. When planting, dig a hole 2' across by 2' deep and fortify the soil with substantial amounts of peat moss or compost so that

moisture will be retained around the roots of the plant. This is essential to vigorous, healthy growth. Virtually carefree once established.

Pruning clematis is a complicated business since some varieties should be cut back to about 1' in late winter and others should merely be pruned to remove dead vines or to shape or contain the plant. It is best to check at point of purchase about pruning the particular variety that you have selected. The same holds true for the varieties' growth habit, which may vary from 3' to 30'. By the way, if you prune your clematis the wrong way you probably won't kill it but you may deprive yourself of blooms for that season.

***Clematis paniculata*** (Sweet autumn clematis) 🐝 🦌
Perennial. Masses of fragrant, small white blossoms in late summer on vigorous, 20–30' tangled vines with attractive, medium-green foliage. Thrives in full sun or partial shade. Drought resistant once established. Plant outdoors in mid-spring. Prune back severely in late fall. A vigorous yet easily controlled plant.

***Hydrangea anomala*** subsp. ***petiolaris*** (Climbing hydrangea) 🐝
Perennial. Large, flat 6–8" white or ivory blossom clusters and attractive deep-green foliage. To 75'. Thrives in enriched soil in partial shade. Requires moisture but is drought resistant once established. Plant outdoors in mid-spring. Usually sold as *Hydrangea petiolaris*. Can be trained to grow up the trunks of tall trees or buildings.

***Ipomoea*** (Morning glory, moonflower)
Annual. Blossoms of sky blue, purple, pink, rose, red, white, or combinations thereof on vigorous vines with heart-shaped, deep-green foliage. Thrives in full sun. Requires moisture. Plant outdoors in situ after all danger of frost, according to package directions. Soak seeds overnight in lukewarm water to hasten germination. The all-time favorite is the lovely 'Heavenly Blue,' which dresses up any garden from midsummer to killing frost. White moonflowers, which bloom in the evening and at night, are ethereal.

Nasturtium

Wisteria

Clematis

Boston ivy

Clematis paniculata

*Lonicera* (Honeysuckle) ❀ ☘

Perennial. A very large genus of plants with many varieties available. All sport delicate, fragrant, spiderlike pink, red, yellow, or white blossoms on vigorous or compact vines with medium-green foliage. Most offer berry displays in the fall. Most thrive in full sun. Plant outdoors from early spring to fall.

*Parthenocissus tricuspidata* (Boston ivy) ❀

Perennial. Ivy-shaped leaves in deep lustrous green that turn brilliant red in the fall on vines up to 35'. Insignificant blue berries in the fall are relished by birds. Thrives in full sun or partial shade. Plant outdoors in mid-spring or fall. Excellent plant for stone walls or facades but will serve as a cover for wooden stockade fences as well.

*Phaseolus coccineus* (Scarlet runner bean)

Annual. Brilliant scarlet, pealike blossoms on 15' vines sporting medium-green foliage. Thrives in full sun or partial shade. Requires moisture. Plant outdoors in situ after all danger of frost. Rapid and strong summer growth make this an ideal plant for sheltered seaside gardens. Train on trellises, posts, or fences.

*Polygonum aubertii* (Silverlace) ❀

Perennial. Panicles of white flowers in late summer on medium-green foliage. To 20". Thrives in sandy soil in full sun. Twining vine grows rapidly but will not harm shingles or wood walls.

*Tropaeolum* (Nasturtium)

Annual. Yellow, orange, gold, and red funnel-shaped blossoms on 3–5' vines bearing pea-green leaves. Thrives in full sun. Requires moisture during drought. Plant seeds outdoors after all danger of frost. Deadhead for continuous bloom. If soil is too rich, foliage will be lush but flowers will be few. The pungent foliage is edible and can be used in salads. In addition to trailing varieties, there are many mounding varieties that can be used in containers, in beds, and for edging.

*Wisteria floribunda/Wisteria sinensis* (Japanese/Chinese wisteria) ☘

Perennial. White, purple, lavender, or pink, highly fragrant blossom clusters, 9–20" long, on vigorous vines to 50', with medium-green loosely structured foliage. Thrives in enriched acidic soil in full sun. Requires moisture during summer drought. Plant in early spring. Avoid fertilizing plant, as this will diminish bloom substantially. Wisteria often needs heavy pruning, particularly if planted on a trellis or pergola adjoining a house or near trees. It has been known to destroy a house if allowed to grow unchecked.

# Water Plants

The following plants are hardy in the North and will winter over in your water garden. Check at point of purchase for planting and growing instructions. Obviously, since these plants grow in water, summer drought is not a problem. Beyond the hardy aquatics, there are many tropical plants that are suitable for water gardens, but be advised that you must provide protection for them throughout the winter. This almost always involves bringing them indoors and wintering them over.

*Acorus calamus* (Sweet flag)

Insignificant flowers on sword-shaped irislike green or green-and-white foliage. 12–30", depending on variety. Thrives in full sun or partial shade in either wet soil or 6" deep water. Grown for foliage. Zone 4.

*Aponogeton distachyus* (Water hawthorne, cape pondweed)

Strange, white vanilla-scented blossoms, green strap-shaped leaves with purple spots. Thrives in partial to moderate shade in containers in 4–12" deep water. Blooms in the spring and fall. Hardy to Zone 5.

*Butomus umbellatus* (Flowering rush)

Modest clusters of three-petaled pink blossoms on rushlike

foliage. 3'. Thrives in full sun in wet soil or water up to 6" deep. Blooms in the summer for two weeks only. Hardy to Zone 6.

*Caltha palustris* (Marsh marigold)
Clusters of large, lustrous yellow buttercuplike blossoms above clumps of deep-green leathery leaves. 1'. Thrives on banks or in containers barely covered by water. Blooms in the spring and often in the fall. Hardy to Zone 5.

*Darmera peltata* (Umbrella plant)
Early spring pink flowers on naked stems to 2', followed by pleated, rounded leaves to 15" across on 4' stems. Spectacular autumn foliage if grown in full sun. Hardy to Zone 4.

*Dulichium arundinaceum* (Dwarf bamboo)
Grown for 1–3' bamboolike stalks of foliage. Thrives in shallow water. Blooms are insignificant. Hardy to Zone 6.

*Eleocharis dulcis* (Chinese water chestnut)
The familiar edible Chinese chestnuts. 1–3' stems with spikes of straw-colored blossoms from summer to fall. Thrives in full sun or partial shade in wet soil or water up to 6" deep. Blooms from summer to fall. Hardy to Zone 7.

*Equisetum hyemale* (Horsetail)
Upright clumps of elegant, fine-textured green stalks with brown stripes at each joint. Brown cones tip the stems. Thrives in partial, not full, sun. Plant above water level on banks of pond. Hardy to Zone 3.

*Iris* (Iris)
A large group of plants suitable for water gardens. All have vertical, graceful, medium-green foliage and sport flamboyant blossoms. If happy, irises will spread into large clumps. Use as vertical accent plants. Foliage is elegant even without flowers. Thrives in boggy soil along banks of water garden or in containers no more than 6" below water surface. Prefers full sun but all varieties flower in partial shade. Varieties available include:

*I. fulva* (Red iris): Small copper red blossoms on bright-green, graceful, narrow foliage. 8–24". Hardy to Zone 5.

*I. pseudacorus* (Yellow flag): Bright-yellow blossoms on tall lance-shaped foliage to 4'. Hardy to Zone 4.

*I. versicolor* (Blue flag): Large blossoms in light to deep blue on sword-shaped leaves to 3'. Blooms from early to mid-spring. Hardy to Zone 4.

*Lotus*
Spectacular large, fragrant, pale yellow, white, deep pink, rose pink, or cream blossoms on enormous circular, deep-green leaves, often 1' across. 2–3'. Blooms early summer to late fall. Locate in area that receives 6 hours of full sun in containers 2–6" below water surface. Hardy to Zones 4 or 5, depending on variety.

*Marsilea* (Water clover)
Grown for 2–3" green or variegated four-leaf-cloverlike foliage. Thrives in partial shade in 4–12" deep water. Hardy to Zone 6.

*Myriophyllum aquaticum* (Parrot's feather)
Fine-textured, blue-green, needlelike foliage. Flowers are insignificant. Thrives in full sun or partial shade in water 4–12" deep. Hardy to Zone 6.

*Nymphaea* (Hardy water lilies)
The most popular aquatic plant of all. Magnificent, large yellow, white, rose, pink, and cream 2–8" blossoms on padlike glossy, leathery foliage. Tropical water lilies, which are not hardy except in warm climates, are available in spectacular blue, purple, pink, rose, yellow, and white. Some are night bloomers. Thrives in full sun in water 6–18" deep. Hardy to Zone 3 or 4.

*Nymphoides cristatum/Nymphoides geminata* (Snowflake)
Charming white or yellow fluffy blossoms on floating foliage. Thrives in full sun or partial shade in water 6" deep. Hardy to Zone 6.

*Orontium aquaticum* (Golden-club)
Gold-tipped white spikes of mini-blossoms on ribbed blue-green waxy foliage. 1". Thrives in partial shade in wet soil or water up to 6" deep. Hardy to Zone 6.

*Peltandra virginica* (Water arum)
Green-and-white jack-in-the-pulpit blossoms on glossy, deep-green, arrow-shaped foliage. 2'. Thrives in full sun or partial shade in boggy soil or up to 6" of water. Hardy to Zone 5.

*Pontederia cordata* (Pickerel rush, pickerel weed)
Spikes of purple, blue, or white blossoms on shiny lancelike foliage. 2–3'. Thrives in full sun or partial shade in water 12" deep. Blooms from midsummer to fall. Hardy to Zone 3.

*Sagittaria latifolia* (Arrowhead)
White three-petaled blossoms on arrow-shaped leaves. 2'. Thrives in full sun or partial shade in boggy soil or water up to 6" deep. Blooms early to late summer. Hardy to Zone 5.

*Saururus cernuus* (Lizard's tail)
Small white blossoms on curved spikes on heart-shaped green foliage. 18". Thrives in full sun or partial shade in wet soil or water up to 6" deep. Hardy to Zone 4.

*Scirpus albescens* (White bulrush)
Grown for foliage and to give a swampy look to a water garden. Cylindrical cream-and-green-striped foliage sports brown tassels in late summer. 2–6'. Thrives in full sun or partial shade, in boggy soil, or in water up to 6" deep. Hardy to Zone 5.

*Typha* (Cattails)
Plump velvet-brown catkins on graceful, slender-leaved foliage. 3–7', depending on variety. Thrives in full sun to partial shade. Hardy from Zones 2 to 5, depending on variety.

Water lily

Lotus

Marsh marigold

# Sources

## BIRD FEEDERS AND SUPPLIES

Droll Yankees, Inc., Foster, RI. Phone: (800) 352-9164; Fax: (401) 647-7620; Internet: www.drollyankees.com. The granddaddy of the bird feeder companies, and still the very best. Prices are fair. An excellent product.

## BULBS

Brent & Becky Bulbs, Gloucester, VA. Phone: (804) 693-3966; Fax: (804) 693-9436; Internet: www.brentandbeckybulbs.com. For the daffodil enthusiast or hobbyist, a wide selection of hard-to-find daffodils is offered.

Van Bourgondien & Sons, Babylon, NY. Phone: (800) 622-9997; Fax: (800) 327-4268; Internet: www.dutchbulbs.com. The largest selection of bulbs available in the United States, and the prices are very reasonable.

## PERENNIAL PLANTS, SHRUBS, AND/OR TREES

Bear Creek Nursery, Northport, WA. Phone: (509) 732-6219; Fax: (509) 732-4417; Internet: www.bearcreeknursery.com. In addition to perennials, this is an excellent source for some of the exciting new annuals.

Bluestone Perennials, Madison, OH. Phone: (800) 852-5243; Internet: www.bluestoneperennials.com. One of the best sources for perennials and shrubs at very reasonable prices.

Great Plant Company, New Hartford, CT. Phone: (860) 379-7495; Fax: (860) 738-2549; Internet: www.greatplants.com. Steve Frowine used to be director of public relations at Burpee Seeds and then at White Flower Farm. He's gone into his own business now, offering very rare plants, suitable for persnickety collectors. Included are lady slipper cultivars from around the world.

Klehm Nursery, Champaign, IL. Phone: (800) 553-3715. A specialty house offering exceptionally beautiful, hard-to-find varieties of peonies, tree peonies, irises, hostas, ornamental grasses, and perennials.

Mellingers, Inc., North Lima, OH. Phone: (800) 321-7444; Fax: (330) 549-3716; Internet: www.mellingers.com. Large variety of seeds and plants, plus extensive selection of basic gardening supplies.

Niche Gardens, Chapel Hill, NC. Phone: (919) 967-0078; Fax: (919) 967-4026; Internet: www.nichegdn.com. Among the many unusual offerings of this house is the hard-to-find native beauty berry.

Schreiner's Iris Gardens, Salem, OR. Phone: (800) 525-2367; Fax: (503) 393-5590; Internet: www.schreinersiris.com. One of the best sources for iris, and the prices are reasonable, except, of course, for new introductions.

Wayside Gardens, Hodges, SC. Phone: (800) 845-1124; Fax: (800) 457-9712; Internet: www.wayside.com. A stunning collection of unusual trees, shrubs, perennials, and roses is offered here. Many rare varieties. Pricey, but worth every penny if you want very special varieties of plants.

Wedge Nursery, Albert Lea, MN. Phone: (507) 373-5225; Fax: (507) 373-2013. One of the best sources for lilacs. Scores of varieties, including many rare cultivars, are offered.

White Flower Farm, Litchfield, CT. Phone: (800) 503-9624; Fax: (860) 411-6159; Internet: www.whiteflowerfarm.com. As always, the best source for Alpine strawberries (fraises des bois) and the purveyor of many other great plants.

## ROSES

Jackson & Perkins, Medford, OR. Phone: (800) 292-4769; Fax: (800) 242-0329; Internet: www.jacksonandperkins.com. Still America's first and foremost source for roses.

SEEDS

The Cook's Garden, Londonderry, VT. Phone: (800) 457-9703; Fax: (800) 457-9705; Internet: www.cooksgarden.com. Wide variety of unusual vegetable seeds, including many French and Italian varieties.

Irish Eyes with a Hint of Garlic, Ellensburg, WA. Phone: (509) 925-6025; Fax: (509) 925-9238; Internet: www.irish-eyes.com. A comprehensive selection of potatoes. Also rhubarb, garlic, shallots, asparagus, sweet potatoes and onion sets.

Johnny's Selected Seeds, Albion, ME. Phone: (207) 437-4395; Fax: (800) 437-4395; Internet: www.johnnyseeds.com. Many foreign vegetable cultivars and heirloom varieties.

Kitazawa Seed Co., San Jose, CA. Phone: (408) 243-1330. One of the few sources for vegetable seeds from East Asia.

Park Seed Co., Inc., Greenwood, SC. Phone: (800) 845-3369; Fax: (800) 275-9941; Internet: www.parkseed.com. The old standby, offering many heirloom vegetable and flower seeds.

Seeds of Distinction, Etobicoke, Canada. Phone: (416) 255-3060; Fax: (888) 327-9193. Seeds for many unusual flowers and vegetables.

Shepherds' Garden Seeds, Torrington, CT. Phone: (860) 482-3638; Fax: (860) 482-0532; Internet: www.shepherdseeds.com. Many unusual offerings for the gourmet gardener.

Thompson & Morgan, Inc., Jackson, NJ. Phone: (800) 274-7333; Fax: (888) 466-4769; Internet: www.thompson-morgan.com. An impressive and remarkable comprehensive collection of vegetable and flower seeds.

Totally Tomatoes, Augusta, GA. Phone: (803) 663-0016; Fax: (888) 477-7333. An amazing array of tomatoes, including many heirloom varieties.

W. Atlee Burpee & Co., Warminster, PA. Phone: (800) 888-1447; Fax: (800) 487-5530; Internet: www.burpee.com. The old standby, now offering heirloom seeds.

WATER GARDENS

Waterford Gardens, Saddle River, NJ. Phone: (201) 327-0721; Fax: (201) 327-0684; Internet: www.waterfordgardens.com. Everything you might need for a fine water garden.

# Acknowledgments

We are very grateful to the following people for their kind assistance in helping us locate beautiful gardens to photograph: Bon and Rosemary Lombardi, Sue Blair, Liz Gordon, Mary-Jane Emmet, L. Herndon Werth, Walter and Harriet Weyer, John Greene, Jay Appelgate, the Reverend Molly Hindman, Corky and Randy Frost, Jan Kirsh, Mrs. Joyce Harris-Stanton, Jane Wait, Oleg and Marielle Bryansky, Ken Ruzicka, Paul Marchese, Pierre Bennerup, Mrs. Francesca P. Irwin, Douglas Jenks, and the late Jean-Patrice Coutraud. We also want to thank the many who offered us kind hospitality while we were on the road visiting gardens: Bets and Moe Trammell of The Little House on Chestnut Street, St. Michaels, Maryland; Tilghman Island Inn, Tilghman Island, Maryland; Linda and Jim McGinnis of Barrow's House, Dorset, Vermont; The Cornucopia of Dorset, Dorset, Vermont; The Village Country Inn, Manchester, Vermont; The Equinox, Manchester Village, Vermont; Carolyn Shook of Wayside Inn, Greenfield Center, New York; Tony and Nancy Melino of Saratoga Rose, Hadley, New York. The following have been particularly helpful in extending assistance: The Netherlands Flower Bulb Information Center, Dansk, Smith & Hawken, and Home Decorator's Collection. Finally, we are most grateful to our editor, Eric Himmel; our designer, Darilyn Carnes; and our dear friend and agent, Roz Cole.

# Index

Italicized page references indicate illustrations.

*Abelia*, 161
*Abies*, 169
*Acer*, 19, 82, 161, 171
*Achillea*, 36, 80, 145, 150
*Acidanthera*, 114, 140
*Aconitum*, 150
*Acorus*, 176
*Adiantum*, 142, 143
*Ageratum*, 129, 154
*Ajuga*, 73, 79, 145, 153
Akebia, 67
*Alchemilla*, 30, 150
*Allium*, 33, 96, 114, 116, 117, 136, 138, 148, see also Onion
Althaea, 165
*Amsonia*, 150
Andromeda, 167
*Anemone*, 84, 128, 136, 150–151
*Anethum*, 148
Angel's trumpet, 131
*Anthemis*, 151
*Antirrhinum*, 129
*Aponogeton*, 176
Apple, 14
*Aquilegia*, 52, 123, 151
*Arabis*, 28, 145
Arborvitae, 168
*Arctotis*, 129
*Arenaria*, 145
*Armeria*, 145
Arrowhead, 178
*Artemisia*, 36, 148, 151
Arugula, 116, 117, 118
*Aruncus*, 151, 153
*Asclepia*, 123, 151

Ash, 172
*Aster*, 130, 151, 152
*Astilbe*, 80, 151
*Athyrium*, 12, 142, 143
*Aubretia*, 28
*Aurinia*, 145–146
Azalea, 13, 19, 20, 52, 63, 110

Baby's breath, 131, 154–155
Bachelor's button, 130
Balloon flower, 80, 158
Balsam, 132
Bamboo, 166–167, 177
*Baptisia*, 151
Barberry, 161
Barrenwort, 46, 146
Basil, 101, 149
Basket of gold, 145–146
Beans, 95, 95, 101, 102, 117–118, 123, 176
Beauty berry, 162
Beauty bush, 166
Bee balm, see *Monarda*
Beech, 172
Beet, 95, 100, 117
*Begonia*, 62, 114, 129
Bellflower, 52, 151
Bells of Ireland, 132
*Berberis*, 161
Bergamot, see *Monarda*
*Betula*, 171–172
Birch, 16, 171–172
Black gum, 173
Black tupelo, 173
Blackberry, 135
Blanket flower, 131, 154
Blazing star, 156
Bleeding heart, 153
Blue plumbago, 146
Bluebeard, 162
Bluebell, 138
Blueberry, 135–136

Bluestar, 150
Bok choy, 117
Bouncing Bet, 158
Box, 161–162
Boxwood, 13
Boysenberry, 135
*Brachycome*, 129
*Brassica* family, 116–117
Broccoli, 101, 117
Broom, 163, 164
*Brunnera*, 82, 151
Brussels sprout, 117
*Buddleia*, 123, 161, 164
Bugbane, 152
Bugleweed, 73, 79, 145, 153
Burkwood daphne, 163
Burning-bush, 163
*Butomus*, 176–177
Butterfly bush, 123, 161
Butterfly milkweed, 123, 151
*Buxus*, 161–162

Cabbage, 100, 117, 118
Caladium, 39, 62, 114
*Calendula*, 46, 108, 129–130
*Callicarpa*, 162
Calliopsis, see *Coreopsis*
*Callistephus*, 130
*Calluna*, 63, 146, 162
*Caltha*, 177, 178
*Camellia*, 23, 103, 162
*Campanula*, 52, 151
*Campsis*, 41, 174
Candytuft, 146
Canna lily, 15, 29, 140
Cape pondweed, 176
Cardinal flower, 123, 156
Carnation, 131
Carrot, 95, 117, 118
*Caryopteris*, 162
Catmint, 149
Catnip, 149

Cattails, 178
Cauliflower, 117, 118
Cedar, 34, 88, 169, 171
*Cedrus*, 34, 88, 169, 171
Celeriac, 116
Celery, 116, 118
*Celosia*, 128, 130
*Centaurea*, 108, 130, 152
*Centranthus*, 152
*Cerastium*, 71, 146
*Ceratostigma*, 146
*Cercis*, 172
*Chaenomeles*, 162
*Chamaecyparis*, 82, 162, 169
*Chamaemelum*, 148–149
Chamomile, 148–149
Chaste tree, 168
Cherries, 15
Cherry, 173
Cherry laurel, 42
*Chionodoxa*, 114, 136
Chive, 148
Christmas rose, 155
*Chrysanthemum*, 14, 16, 43, 80, 100, 113, 152
*Chrysopsis*, 152
*Cimicifuga*, 35, 152
Cinquefoil, 167
*Clematis*, 35, 38, 92, 174, 175
*Cleome*, 20–21, 25, 43, 90, 128, 130
*Clethra*, 162
Cockscomb, 130
*Colchicum*, 142
*Coleus*, 18–19, 81, 130
Columbine, 52, 123, 151
Coneflower, 62, 66, 123, 153–154, 158
*Consolida*, 130
*Convallaria*, 20, 114, 124, 136
*Coprosma*, 68–69
Coralbells, 155

*Coreopsis, 14, 43, 66, 130, 152*
Corn, 117
Cornflower, 130
*Cornus, 63, 121, 163, 170, 172*
*Cortaderia, 143*
*Corydalis, 17, 29, 34, 152*
*Cosmos, 43, 123, 130–131*
*Cotinus, 163*
*Cotoneaster, 163*
Crab apple, 121, 123, 173
Cranesbill, *89*
Crape myrtle, 166
*Crataegus, 172*
Cress, 116, 117, 118, 145
*Crocosmia, 123, 138, 140*
*Crocus, 114, 124–125, 126, 136, 138, 142*
Crown imperial, 124, 137
*Cryptomeria, 169*
Cucumber, 117–118, *118*
Currant, 134, *135*
Cushion spurge, 154
Cypress, false, *82*, 162, 169
*Cytisus, 163, 164*

Daffodil, *52, 84, 104*, 114, 115, 116, 124, 125, 137–138, *138*, 142
Dahlia, 114, 115
Daisy, *14, 16, 43, 62, 80, 100*, 129, 131, 151, 152
*Daphne, 163*
*Darmera, 86*, 177
*Datura, 131*
Daylily, *16, 17, 22, 24, 36*, 115, 155
Dead nettle, 146
*Delphinium, 30*, 130, 152
*Deutzia, 79, 163*
Dewberry, 135
*Dianthus, 118, 131, 153*
*Dicentra, 153*
*Digitalis, 153*
Dill, 148

Dogwood, *63*, 121, 163, *170*, 172
Donkey tail, *44*
*Doronicum, 153*
*Dulichium, 177*
Dusty miller, 133, 151
*Dyssodia, 131*

Echeveria, 28
*Echinacea, 123, 153–154*
*Echinops, 154*
Eggplant, 117–118, *118*
*Elaeagnus, 172*
*Eleocharis, 177*
*Epimedium, 46, 146*
*Equisetum, 177*
*Eranthis, 136*
*Erica carnea, 146*
*Eryngium, 154*
*Eschscholzia, 131*
*Euonymus, 31, 146, 163*
*Eupatorium, 154*
*Euphorbia, 154*

*Fagus, 172*
Fantail, 79
Fennel, 123
Fern, *12*, 20, 24, 50, 108, 142–143, *143, 143*
Fescue grass, 42, 143
*Festuca, 42*, 143
Feverfew, *93*
*Filipendula, 35*, 154
Fir, 169
Flax, 156
Forget-me-not, *82*, 151
*Forsythia, 163*
Forth, 114
*Fothergilla, 165*
Fountain grass, 144, *144*
Foxglove, 153
*Fragaria, 134*
Fraises des bois, 134

Frankin tree, *170*, 172
*Frankinia, 170*, 172
*Fraxinus, 172*
*Fritillaria, 124, 136, 137*
Fuchsia, *18–19*

*Gaillardia, 131, 154*
*Galanthus, 114, 124, 125, 137, 138*
*Gallium, 19, 25, 149*
Garlic, *96*, 116, 117, 148
Gay-feather, 156
Geranium, see *Pelargonium*
Geranium, 89
*Geum, 154*
Ginger, 79
*Gladiolus, 114, 140–141*
*Gleditsia, 172*
Glory-of-the-snow, 114, 136
Goatsbeard, 151
Gold dust, 145–146
Golden-chain tree, 173
Golden-club, 178
Goldenrod, 158
Gooseberry, 134, *135*
Grape, *102*
Grass, *15, 20, 42, 44, 73*, 143–144, *144*
Guinea hen flower, 137
*Gypsophila, 131, 154–155*

*Hamamelis, 165, 170*
Hawthorn, 172
Heath, 146
Heather, *63*, 146, 162
*Hebe, 165*
*Hedera, 146*
*Helenium, 155*
*Helianthus, 128, 131*
*Helichrysum, 131*
*Heliopsis, 107*, 155
Heliotrope, *128*, 131

*Heliotropium, 128*, 131
Helix, *90*
*Helleborus, 155*
*Hemerocallis*, see Daylily
Hemlock, 168
Hemp tree, 168
Hens and chickens, *17*, 147
*Heuchera, 34*, 155
*Hibiscus, 155*, 165
*Holcus, 143, 144*
Holly, 105, 169
Honeysuckle, *51*, 176
Horsetail, 177
*Hosta, 12, 16, 18–19, 22, 24, 37, 39, 52, 57, 61, 62, 82, 83*, 155
Hyacinth, 114–115, 137
Hybrid witchhazel, 165
*Hydrangea, 23, 24, 42, 61, 79, 83*, 165, *165*, 174
*Hypericum, 146*, 165

*Iberis, 146*
*Ilex, 169*
*Impatiens, 12, 13, 37, 39, 45, 47, 81*, 123, 132
*Imperata, 143–144*
Indigo, 151
*Iris, 54, 80, 82, 83*, 114, 118, 120, 124, 137, 153, 155–156, 177
Ivy, *23, 30, 61, 62*, 146, *175*, 176

Jacob's ladder, 147
Japanese bloodgrass, 143–144
Japanese snowdrop tree, 174
Joe-Pye weed, 154
Juniper, 165–166, 171
*Juniperus, 165–166, 171*

*Kalmia, 166*
*Kerria, 166*
Kidney bean, 117
*Kniphofia, 153, 156*

Kohlrabi, 117
*Kolkwitzia*, 166

*Laburnum*, 48–49, 173
Lady's mantle, 30, 150
*Lagerstroemia*, 166
Lamb's ear, 145, 149–150
*Lamium*, 62, 145, 146
Lantana, 88, 123
Larkspur, 130
Lavender, 66, 93, 100, 149
Lavender cotton, 149
*Lavendula*, 66, 93, 100, 149
Leek, 116
Lenten rose, 155
Leopard's bane, 153
Lettuce, 98, 101, 116, 117, 118
*Leucojum*, 137
*Leucothoe*, 166
*Liatris*, 156
*Ligularia*, 156
*Ligustrum*, 166
Lilac, 110, 123, 161, 168
Lily, 15, 29, 36, 43, 80, 114, 115, 118, 138, 140, 141
Lily of the valley, 20, 114, 124, 136
Lily, water, *see Nymphaea*
Lilyturf, 146
Lima bean, 95, 102, 117
*Limonium*, 132
*Linum*, 156
*Liriope*, 146
Lizard's tail, 178
*Lobelia*, 46, 108, 123, 132, 156
*Lobularia*, 46, 132
Locust, 172, 173
Loganberry, 135
*Lonicera*, 51, 176
Loosestrife, 64, 156, 157
*Lotus*, 57, 60–61, 79, 84, 120, 177, 178

Love-in-a-mist, 132
Lungwort, 158
Lupine, 36, 156
*Lupinus*, 36, 156
*Lychnis*, 156
*Lysimachia*, 64, 156, 157
*Lythrum*, 16, 22, 82, 83, 157

*Magnolia*, 22, 166, 173
Maiden grass, 15
Mallow, 123, 155, 157
*Malus*, 173
*Malva*, 36, 80, 123, 157
Maple, 13, 57, 79, 82, 161, 171
Marguerite, 151
Marigold, 89, 96, 100, 108, 112–113, 123, 177, 178
Marigold, pot, *see Calendula*
Marrow, 94
*Marsilea*, 177
*Matteuccia*, 142, 143
*Matthiola*, 132
Meadow rue, 159
Melon, 117–118, 118
*Menthe*, 149
Mexican shell flower, 141
Michael's flower, 137
Michaelmas daisy, 151
Milkweed, 123
Mint, 149
*Miscanthis*, 83
*Miscanthus*, 144
Mock orange, 167
*Moluccella laevis*, 132
*Monarda*, 14, 80, 101, 123, 153, 157
Mondo grass, 73
Monkshood, 150
Montbretia, 123, 138, 140
Moon flower, 41, 174
Morning glory, 41, 174
Moss, 12, 72–73

Moss pink, 84, 123, 147
Moss sandwort, 145
Mountain laurel, 166
*Muscari*, 114, 137, 138
Mustard, 116, 118
*Myriophyllum*, 79, 177
Myrtle, 147, 166

*Nandina*, 166–167
*Narcissus, see* Daffodil
Nasturtium, 46, 94, 175, 176
*Nepeta*, 80, 149
*Nephrolepsis*, 50
*Nicotiana*, 43, 44, 132
*Nigella*, 132
*Nyassa*, 173
*Nymphaea*, 54, 57, 60–61, 79, 84, 87, 118, 120, 177, 178
*Nymphoides*, 120, 177

Oak, 173
Obedient plant, 158
*Ocimum*, 101, 149
*Oenothera*, 157
Olive, 172
Onion, 100, 116, 117, *see also Allium*
Orange butterfly weed, 151
Orchid, 140
Oregano, 149
*Origanum*, 149
*Orontium*, 178
*Osmunda*, 142
Oswego tea, *see Monarda*

*Pachysandra*, 13, 20, 145, 147
*Paeonia*, 157, 164, 167
Painted tongue, 133
Palm, 54
Pampas grass, 143
*Panicum*, 144
Pansy, 25, 62

*Papaver*, 157
Parrot's feather, 79, 177
Parsley, 123
*Parthenocissus*, 23, 175, 176
Pasqueflower, 150–151
Pea, 116, 118
Pear, 38
Peckerel rush, 178
*Pelargonium*, 46, 47, 89, 132–133
*Peltandra*, 178
*Pennisetum*, 44, 81, 144, 144
Penstemon, 123
Peony, 157, 164, 167
Pepper, 117–118, 118
Pepperridge, 173
Periwinkle, 147
*Perovskia*, 157
Persian bell, 137
*Petunia*, 44, 46, 51, 65, 90, 123
*Phaseolus*, 123, 176
*Philadelphus*, 167
*Phlox*, 31, 39, 80, 84, 123, 147, 153, 157
*Physostegia*, 158
*Picea*, 87, 106, 167, 171
*Pieris*, 167
Pincushion flower, 133
Pine, 87, 88, 171
Pinks, 118, 131, 153
*Pinus*, 87, 88, 171
Plaintain lily, *see Hosta*
*Platycodon*, 31, 80, 158
Plum, 173
Pole bean, 95
*Polemonium*, 147
*Polianthes*, 141
*Polygonatum*, 158
*Polygonum*, 176
*Polypodium*, 143
*Pontederia*, 178
Poppy, 107, 131, 157

Portulaca, *90*, 133
Potato, *102*
*Potentilla,* 167
Primrose, *58–59,* 157, 158
*Primula, 58–59,* 158
Privet, 166
*Prunus, 15, 42,* 173
*Pulmonaria, 39, 52,* 158
Pumpkin, *76–77,* 117–118
Purple coneflower, 123, 153–154
*Puschkinia,* 138
*Pyracantha,* 167

Queen-of-the-prairie, *35,* 154
*Quercus,* 173
Quince, 162

Radish, 116, 117, 118
Ragwort, 156
Raspberry, 135
Red valerian, 152
Redbud, 172
*Rhododendron, 19, 58–59,* 110,
    167, *see also* Azalea
*Ribes,* 134, *135*
*Robinia,* 173
Rock cress, 145
Rose, *72, 100,* 118, 155, 156, 159–
    161, *160,* 166
Rose of Sharon, 165
*Rubus,* 135
*Rudbeckia, 15, 62, 66,* 158
Rush, 176–177

Sage, 123, 149, 157, 158
*Sagittaria,* 178
Saint-John's-wort, 146, 166
*Salix,* 173–174
*Salpiglossis,* 133
Salsify, 116
*Salvia, 15,* 123, 133, 149, 158
*Santolina,* 149

*Saponaria, 28,* 158
*Saururus cernuus,* 178
*Scabiosa,* 133
Scallion, *98*
Scarlet firehorn, 167
Scarlet runner bean, 123, 176
*Scilla,* 114, 125, 138, 139
*Scirpus,* 178
Sea holly, 154
*Sedum, 15, 20–21, 25, 28, 29, 31,
    44, 72–73, 82,* 147
*Sempervivum,* 147
*Senecio,* 133, 156
Shallot, 116
Silverlace, 176
Slender deutzia, 163
Smokebush, 163
Snakeroot, 152
Snapdragon, 129
Sneezeweed, 155
Snow-in-summer, *71,* 146
Snowbell, 174
Snowdrop, 114, 124, 125, 137
Snowflake, 120, 177
*Solidago,* 158
Solomon's seal, 158
Sour gum, 173
Speedwell, 147, 159
Spider flower, *see Cleome*
Spinach, 116, 117
*Spiraea,* 167–168
*Spirea,* 164
Spruce, *87,* 106, 167, 171
Squash, *98, 101,* 117–118, *118*
Squill, 138, 139
*Stachys,* 145, 149–150
Statice, 132
*Sternbergia,* 142
Stock, 132
*Stokesia,* 158
Stonecrop, *see Sedum*
Strawberry, 134

Strawflower, 131
String bean, *101,* 117
*Styrax, 83,* 174
Summer-sweet, 162
Sunflower, 123, *128,* 131, 134, 155
Sweet alyssum, *46,* 132
Sweet flag, 176
Sweet pepperbush, 162
Sweet woodruff, *19, 25,* 149
Swiss chard, 117
Switch grass, 144
*Syringa,* 110, 168

*Tagetes, see* Marigold
Tarragon, 148
*Taxus,* 168
*Thalicritum,* 159
*Thelypteris,* 143
Thistle, 154
Thrift, 145
*Thuja,* 168
Thyme, *73,* 150
*Thymus, 73,* 150
Tiger flower, 141
*Tigridia,* 114, 141
*Tithonia,* 123, 134
Tobacco plant, *43, 44,* 132
Tomato, 95, *96, 98, 101,* 116, 117–
    118
Torch flower, *153,* 156
*Tropaeolum, 46, 94, 175,* 176
Trumpet vine, *41,* 174
Tuberose, 141
Tulip, 104, 114–115, *115,* 124–125,
    126, 139–140
*Tulipa, see* Tulip
*Typha,* 178

Umbrella plant, *86,* 177

*Vaccinium,* 135–136
Velvet flower, 133

Velvet grass, 143, *144*
*Verbascum,* 159
*Verbena, 44, 90,* 134
*Veronica,* 147, 159
*Viburnum,* 168
*Vinca,* 147
*Vitex,* 168

Water arum, 178
Water chestnut, 177
Water clover, 177
Water hawthorne, 176
Water lily, *see Nymphaea*
Watercress, *81*
*Weigela,* 169
White bulrush, 178
Willow, 173–174
Winged euonymus, 163
Winter aconite, 136
Winter creeper, 146
*Wisteria, 175,* 176
Witchhazel, 165, *170*
Wreath, 167–168

Yarrow, *36, 80,* 145, 150
Yew, 168
*Yucca,* 159

*Zantedeschia,* 141
Zebra grass, *15*
Zinnia, *32, 36, 90,* 123, 134